Volunteers for Peace

Field reports on relief work in Europe
1944 to 1949
By
International Voluntary Service for Peace
(I.V.S.)

Compiled and edited by
Basil Eastland, Derek Edwards & David Sainty
with Illustrations by Jill Slee Blackadder

D1342293

Curlew Productions

© Basil Eastland, Derek Edwards & David Sainty

Published in May 1998
Curlew Productions • Kelso, Scotland TD5 8PD

ISBN 1 900259 08 7

Cover design by David Woolgrove

Illustrations by Jill Slee Blackadder

Typesetting & design by *Curlew Productions*, Kelso TD5 8PD
Set in Adobe Garamond 11/13.2.
Printed by *Kelso Graphics*, Kelso TD5 7BH

in memoriam
Derek Edwards
15th January 1915 — 18th October 1994
IVSP Foreign Service Secretary 1943 to 1949
and General Secretary

Basil Eastland
BA(Mus.) (Reading) LRAM ARCM
4th August 1920 — 7th September 1996

Acknowledgments

My late colleagues and I have received much willing help. The cost of printing of this publication has been funded by the Rowntree Charitable Trust. The contributors not only provided their notes and diaries and correspondence but gave the Editors *carte blanche* to use such parts as they thought appropriate. In the search for Ernst (Prologue) Fred Roberts and Bessie Latham produced valuable information, and many people unconnected with IVSP promptly answered requests, notably the Bishop of Lichfield and Prebendary Lawson, the Imperial War Museum, and Mr. John Cox, lately archivist to the Earl of Verulam (Jim Forrester, 5th Earl, was an early and active volunteer with IVSP). Peter Bramham, son of Ramsay who died in 1954, gave practical help in the early stages of preparing the MS, and Jill Slee Blackadder, daughter of Stan Slee who died in 1992, readily agreed to draw the illustrations, which in spite of other commitments she delivered by the deadline. David Woolgrove undertook the publishing and distribution and contributed his expertise in tackling an unusual assignment, and drawing the maps and designing the cover. On behalf of my colleagues in this work, (who both died of cancer after we had experienced an unusual and happy form of re-union half a century on), and myself, I express thanks to all who have helped.

David L Sainty

Contents

PROLOGUE

In 1933, IVSP commenced work on the longest and largest of its projects in the UK. This was to remove the Charlton Mound, a huge tip resulting from iron mining carried out in OAKENGATES in Shropshire. Not only was the mound unsightly, but it blocked daylight from the lower windows of a row of houses, and the plan was for the cleared site to be used for various community facilities. It had been originally estimated that some 60,000 tons would need to be cleared, but in fact when the project finished in 1939 it was thought that at least 80,000 tons had been removed. The IVSP history records that 500-600 volunteers took part in these services, coming from many countries, including Germany.

The site is now occupied by an Old People's Home, named "Cartlidge House" after Rev. Gordon Cartlidge, vicar of Oakengates Holy Trinity Church, who had promoted the clearance plan and invited IVSP to undertake the work. (DE)

THE RAID

Letter to Shropshire Star Mail, 5/11/81:

"The article (Shropshire Star, October 27) about the lady from Ironbridge who witnessed the attempted power station bombing brought back memories of a similar incident at St Georges.

"We were young teenage boys. It was either 1940 or 1941. We had just finished playing football on St George's Rec.

"We were sitting on the railings round the old cycle track, changing from our football boots. It was just about dusk when suddenly we heard an aircraft.

"Looking up we saw a bomber approaching from the west side of the church tower. Hearing the drone of its engines, I shouted out: 'It's a Jerry.' 'Don't be soft,' said my mates, including my brother Doug, who at the time was the champion plane spotter.

"When the bomber got nearly overhead I was proved to be right. We could see its German markings. It then banked to its left and headed towards the back side of the rec. Within a split second it dropped its bombs.

"There was a big flash and explosion. The bomber, which, if I remember rightly, was a Junkers 88, revved its engines and made a steep climb to escape the blast and flew off towards the Shropshire / Staffordshire border leaving us in a state of fright and excitement. Two men, one of whom was my elder brother Jim, came across from the bowling green and told us to get off home.

"We heard later that it had been shot down in Staffordshire. The rumour was that the pilot had been one of the international workers who had been employed on removing the old Charlton Mount at Oakengates just before the war."

Derek Rushton, Ketley Bank

THE PILOT WHO WAVED

Letter to Shropshire Star, 19/11/81:

"I well remember the day the bombs fell in the Lodge Woods, St. Georges. That afternoon my sister and I were walking our dogs on what were then Plant's Fields when we heard the noise of a German plane. Looking up we saw the swastika on the plane just a few feet above us and the pilot, in his helmet and goggles, looked down and waved.

"At that time the Germans were strafing civilians too, so, scared stiff we dived under some bushes. The plane passed over Holy Trinity Church, Oakengates, and headed for St Georges.

"A minute or so later the whole area shook as the bombs fell. We dashed home to find several ornaments broken on the floor.

"Our late vicar told us later about the pilot's connection with the IVSP which had its headquarters in the old Holy Trinity Institute. The pilot told him that his target was C.O.D. Donnington and also said he could have wiped out Oakengates that afternoon, but couldn't bomb the many friends he had made before the war, so dropped his bombs in the Lodge Wood instead."

Mrs. G. Weaver, Ketley Bank

Letter to Shropshire Star, 29/11/81:

"Derek Rushton's letter has sparked off a whole series of memories. Firstly I wrote myself. My letter caused Mrs. Bessie Latham of St Georges, who, like Mrs. Weaver, had witnessed these falling bombs, to write to me personally telling me she had been an employee of the late Rev. Gordon Cartlidge, the man who befriended the international campers, and had met many of them, including the late Pierre Ceresole - a 'giant' of a man was her comment.

"Which of the several German volunteers who worked on the Charlton Mound was the bomber pilot?"

Miss Celia Radcliffe, Shrewsbury

Letter to Bernard Pike, 25/11/81:

"Derek Rushton, whom I don't know, said that from two separate sources he has heard the pilot's name was Ernst - perhaps Müller or something like that. He said he had been to see Mrs. Weaver and had discussed the incident with her and had found the date was 28th September 1940.

Amitié,
Celia"

A PEACE HERO

Letter to Celia Radcliffe, 5/1/82:

"My friend, Mr. Rushton, passed on your letter to me to read. The story starts when I was a young boy - 12 or 13 years old. We were told that foreign students were coming to level what we knew as the Charlton Mount. On several occasions my friends and I played truant from school to work with them. At one time I knew them all by name. Even to this day one or two names still linger in my memory. If my memory serves me right a man named Pierre was in charge. I think he was Swiss. And a lady called Clara and two or three other ladies, and Ernst the German - a tall well built man. People round here used to marvel at his strength - strong as an ox.

"When they had settled down they used to entertain the people of Oakengates by giving weekly concerts and organising hikes. Many times I've been to the Wrekin with them and around the country.

"I was called up for 6 years. When I arrived home, after 3 years abroad of course, we had a family get together. It was during our party I was talking to my uncle about what had happened whilst I had been away, and he told me of a scare they had experienced, saying one of these students that used to work on the Charlton Mount had come over and dropped his bombs in the Lodge Wood, about one and a half miles from Oakengates.

"I thought nothing else of it until about 4 or 5 years ago when I went to see the Rev Gordon Cartlidge. I had not seen Mr. Cartlidge for about 30 years. I spent a good 2 hours talking of old times with him, and then he said 'Fred' - he had not forgotten my name - 'you remember the IVSP'. I said I did. He said Ernst became a German pilot and had come over one evening and dropped his bombs in the Lodge Wood, and was shot down, was wounded and taken to hospital. Whilst there he asked them to contact Rev. Cartlidge at Oakengates. They did and Mr. Cartlidge said he went to see him, and Ernst told him that his target had been the Depot at Donnington but would not bomb it on account of all the friends he had made at Oakengates and still thought of them as his friends.

"Although I was in Italy or Africa at the time, had Ernst bombed the Depot thousands of people would have died. Secretly in my heart I look upon Ernst as a Hero."

Mr. F.B.Roberts, Oakengates.

L'AMITIÉ

Letter to Bernard Pike, 10/1/82:
`"It was a delight talking to Mr. Roberts on the phone - he said all sorts of little things had come back into his head, such as the tune of the song to open activities - I nearly sang it into the phone, but can't sing in tune!

Amitié, Celia"

L'Amitié
Usually the first verse was sung, with hands linked, before and after work; all verses at the beginning and end of the "Service" [project].

Toi qui fais de nos misères
Disparaître la moitié,
Viens nous faire vivre en frères,
Charme pur de l'Amitié!

Quel spectacle sur la terre
Si le monde aimait tes lois!
Plus de troubles, plus de guerres
Et la Paix sous tous les toits!

Parles aux âmes trop altières
Et les soumets à ta loi;
Viens ranger sous ta bannière
Et les peuples et les rois.

THE SEARCH FOR ERNST

Extensive enquiries from 1994 to 1996 have failed to produce the essential piece of information which would lead to identification of Ernst. Everyone in IVSP was on first-name terms and those few still alive who knew Ernst never heard his surname.

The fact that Bessie Latham acted as housekeeper to Mr. Cartlidge suggested that he was a bachelor, and it was a fair guess that he kept a diary. So he was and so he did - the Bishop of Lichfield kindly asked Rev. Prebendary C.J.Lawson to investigate, and a nephew of Mr. Cartlidge produced to Mr. Lawson the information that his uncle kept a diary from 1918 until the 1970s, but although he was asked by various bodies to bequeath the diary to them, he refused because it was written for himself only, and he burned the 50-odd volumes in the early 70s. It is certain that Ernst's identification could have been established from that diary: other sources had to be tried.

The IVSP History published in 1948 includes a photograph of four volunteers working at Oakengates, the caption to which notes that 2 were American, 1 Swiss and 1 German. When a copy of this photo was sent to Fred Roberts with no caption and the question whether he recognised any one in the photo he replied that after 60 years it was difficult to be certain of one's memory, but that the fourth was, he thought, Ernst. A life-size portrait was 'realised', Fred supplying clear information on several aspects of Ernst's appearance which were doubtful in the tiny photo. This is the nearest we can come at this time to an identification, but it has been of no practical use thus far.

The Ministry of Defence replied through a Minister that it had no information which might lead to Ernst but suggested other lines of enquiry.

The Public Records Office provided particulars of the searches which could be made there. Neither time nor funds have been available to follow this up: later indications (below) suggest that such time and expense might have been wasted.

The Red Cross would have given all the help they could,

but without a surname it was impossible to gain access to International Red Cross PoW records.

The Imperial War Museum was exceptionally helpful, but could find no record of any air activity over Britain on 28/9/40 or any other date in 1940, nor - in case the date was misremembered - in 1941.

At this point the possibility started to emerge that the aborted raid might have been officially inconvenient; and this became a probability when Mrs. Bessie Latham confirmed that the bomb explosion in Lodge Wood happened shortly after she had had her first baby, born 1/9/40.

A volunteer Aircraft Recovery Group offered to investigate and report back; but no further communication was received.

On 26/7/96 the Guardian carried a reference to a Whitehall wartime code-name 'Rainy Day' which effectively wiped from all records any events which might damage or weaken civilian morale.

So, unless further information comes to light, we are left with the following:

1. Knowledge that the raid intended for COD Donnington but aborted to Lodge Wood took place.

2. Knowledge that the pilot had worked as a volunteer at the Oakengates workcamp some time between 1933 and 1939.

3. Knowledge that the pilot was shot down and hospitalised at Cosford and thereafter transferred to a PoW camp.

4. Deduction that aborting the raid would be a (capital?) Court Martial offence.

5. Supposition that German Intelligemce would not lose sight of Ernst.

6. Supposition that German Intelligence would penetrate all PoW camps.

7. Supposition that British Intelligence priorities would not include protection of an expendable German.

8. Finally, the speculation that Ernst's having been sent on the COD mission was not a coincidence, as was assumed by some of the few IVSP members who heard of the incident after 1980; but if not, Ernst started out as a spy: and ended ... as a martyr?

A relevant footnote can be added:

In 1935 Rev. J.E. Gordon Cartlidge FRHistS Hon CF published privately by subscription a history of Oakengates from the earliest times. Chapter X was titled War and Peace Memorials and pp 116/9 were taken up with an account of IVSP and its work in Oakengates: Mr. Cartlidge clearly regarded it (then only halfway through) as a Peace Memorial. Six years later Ernst made his decision.

PREFACE

DEVELOPMENTS LEADING TO IVSP[†]
UNDERTAKING OVERSEAS CIVILIAN RELIEF WORK
FOLLOWING THE SECOND WORLD WAR

Derek Edwards

When war broke out in September 1939 SCI[†] had small national branches or groups in Norway, Sweden, Czechoslovakia, Austria, Great Britain, Holland, Belgium, France and Switzerland. Their work was co-ordinated by an International Secretariat in Switzerland. The war, of course, brought a temporary end to SCI services.

In Great Britain, alternative service for conscientious objectors to military service had been recognised to a degree in the first world war and in a debate in the House of Commons soon after the outbreak of war on the treatment of C.O.s the work of IVSP[†] (British branch of SCI) was described by Edmund Harvey MP (brother of Professor John Harvey, Chairman of IVSP).

This led to an invitation from the Government to IVSP to consider undertaking forestry services as an alternative to military training for C.O.s.

Such an invitation was encouraging as it recognised the status and responsibility of the movement and it was with regret and after long discussion that it was decided that, if IVSP was to accept this invitation, it would have to stipulate conditions which the Executive Committee felt sure would be refused by the Government; but the Government's quite quick acceptance of all the conditions was received and in 1940 the first IVSP Forestry

† *(IVSP) International Voluntary Service for Peace*
  (SCI) Service Civil International

service opened at Hawkshead. In order to underline the international principle of SCI services a Swiss, Willi Begert, was invited to be its first leader. Willi Begert had led the latter stages of the relief service in the Spanish Civil War and had also worked in the International Secretariat.

This was, in effect, the first time a government had recognised international voluntary service as an alternative to military service, which was one of the main aims of the founders of SCI, and I have seen a letter written to Jean Inebnit (Honorary Secretary of IVSP) from Pierre Ceresole [the Swiss member of the International Fellowship of Reconciliation who founded SCI and who, along with his brother Ernest, organised the first services of SCI] complaining of the delay in getting this news to him and saying there should be a celebration "from the top of a mountain"!

IVSP AND THE COUNCIL OF BRITISH SOCIETIES FOR RELIEF ABROAD

Very soon after 'Dunkirk' and the evacuation from Europe of all the Allied Forces the British Government began to make plans to deal with the civilian relief work that would be needed when the Allies opened their 'Second Front'. It was recognised that the experience of the various voluntary organisations in this field would make them well qualified to undertake this work but it decided that it could not deal directly with every organisation that might wish to take part.

The Council of British Societies for Relief Abroad (COBSRA) was set up to represent all the voluntary bodies, who would operate under the 'umbrella' of the British Red Cross Society. There were, however, some conditions of membership of COBSRA which to SCI eyes were encouraging and progressive. Only those bodies were eligible for membership "which were organised internationally in more than one country outside the British Commonwealth of Nations" or which had "national counterparts".

These were conditions which IVSP could of course comply with but compared with other organisations such as the Red Cross, the St. Johns Ambulance, Save the Children Fund, etc., it was a very tiny, under resourced, little known organisation with a title that in the middle of a war could be expected to raise official eyebrows to record heights!

COBSRA had also been involved in relief work in the Spanish Civil War and the scale and the quality of the work undertaken by SCI had been observed by a number of influential bodies and individuals. The result was the happy one of an invitation to become a member of COBSRA and a Foreign Service office (given to IVSP rent free by Toc H) at 10 Deans Yard, Westminster, SW1 was set up to administer this new branch of IVSP service.

Two conditions had been laid down by Government for accepting members of relief teams. The first was that only British nationals could be selected, and it has to be recognised that for a Government in the middle of a war this was understandable as it was envisaged that relief teams would be close to the 'front' where 'security' would be a factor. The second condition imposed for the same reasons as the first, was that the members of the relief teams although civilians would be required to wear khaki uniforms. IVSP and some other organisations were not happy about these conditions and it was suggested to IVSP that whilst it was fruitless at this stage to try and get the 'only British' rule lifted in general terms, an application that could be made on strong grounds for a specific individual might receive sympathetic consideration.

IVSP shoulder badge

Edhessa

Thessaloníki

Kozani

Aliakmon

Gjirokaster

Ag.Dimitrios
Kokkinopilos
Mt Olympus
Deskati Likoudi Kalivia
Krania Olympia
Valanida Stormion
Elasson Kokkino Nero
Kalambaka Tsaritsani
Domeniko
Megalo Khorio Tirnavos
Trikkala Lárisa

Mt Athos

Moúdhros

KÉRKIRA
(Corfu)

Ioánnina

AEGEAN SEA

Kardhitsa Vólos

Farsala

Prevesa
Vonitza Amphilochia
Lefkas Mytikas

KALAMOS

Astakos Agrínion

Aitolikon Amfissa Delphi
Ithaka Missolongion

Khalkís

Argostolion
KEFALLINIA
(Cephalonia)

Patrai

Kalavrita

Athens

Salamis

Piraíevs

Zákinthos
(Zante)

Alfios

Argos Navplion

IONIAN SEA

Kalamáta
Sparta

**MIRTOAN
SEA**

Kíthira

Khaniá

CRETE Iráklion

0   50   100 Miles

0   50   100   150 Kilometres

RELIEF ABROAD I

MIDDLE EAST, GREECE, CRETE & ITALY

The first request to IVSP was to send teams to the Middle East. The leader of the team which went to Greece was none other than Willi Begert who having started the Hawkshead service was not able to return to Switzerland as Europe had been occupied in the meantime. There could hardly have been a stronger case to make for a specific foreign national to break the "British only" rule and permission was duly given. This enabled other organisations to make similar requests which were granted, and IVSP also sent other foreign nationals later.

It should be emphasised that SCI has always been a peace movement but not a *pacifist* one. The early camps were organised jointly by Pierre Ceresole, a pacifist, and his brother Ernest, a Colonel in the Swiss army. In wartime, non-pacifist members were by and large in the armed forces *(see Derek Edwards' report in Preface to Journal, p 119)* and those available for relief work tended therefore to be Conscientious Objectors.

Team members were not selected for any specialist qualifications. Sometimes, however, their interests found natural slots in their work. Bay Hyde's founding of the International Club in Guildford led to the International Club in Duisburg; Norman Lancashire's Esperanto enthusiasm led to an Esperanto Club; Beryl Verling-Brown's qualifications as a "Feeding Scheme Expert" were obviously needed. And so on. Each volunteer received 10/- [50p] per week.

THE FIRST UNITS

IVSP initially selected three Units that were on stand-by for the call to go overseas. This did not come until early 1944 when IVSP was one of the organisations invited to contribute a Unit to go out with the first "wave" to the refugee camps in the Middle East, then on to Greece, Italy or Yugoslavia when these countries were no longer under military occupation.

The assembly point for the departure of COBSRA's first wave on February 19th 1944 was the IVSP Foreign Service Office in Dean's Yard.

Two other Units followed during the next few months. All the Units spent some time in the Middle East before Unit 1 was sent into Greece early in December 1944. Unit 2 followed on into Crete and then later to Greece, and Unit 3 was posted to Italy.

DE

Cairo fruit seller

EGYPT

Diary, [Middle East & Greece]   *Douglas Lascelles (Unit 1)*

Sat. 19 Feb 1944
...we left Aldenham and reached Dean's Yard late because of train holdup. A dash over to Schmidtz, Charlotte St. followed, a meagre tea there, and then Donald Wolfit in Richard III — very amateurish; one scene-shifter left hanging in air over stage as he clung to raised scenery. Dean's Yard again to join up with RC and St. J., eat, hear from Sir Wm Goode, and prepare to depart.

Piled into 3 army lorries, and, in wonder and amaze, were driven quickly and secretively to Kings Cross where we were bustled into a special train with locked doors and mysterious serial letters. At 12.40 am we moved out into the darkness of a dark future.

Sun. 20th
Slow arrival at Liverpool docks, 20 standing stops in various cold places, customs a mere formality; at last up the gangway and aboard a ship standing where the dear little Douglas steamer used to berth. Charles [Lindsay: Senior Representative] to cabin, we to E.7, crowded and comfortless ...standing out into the Mersey this evening along with other transports.

Wed. 23
...heading SSW to S ...rumour of sub...

Thurs. 24
...swinging S to SE...

Tues. 29
...I slipped out, and there was Africa, the first land for 10 days and a vision of colour and form.

March 6
...arrived...we land tomorrow. The water was a pale green this morning. We were approaching the Nile Delta. We saw pure white cones on the horizon, like small intensely white table napkins. Native fishing boats. Then we saw the city, flat and colourful... we disembark at Port Said.

REFUGEE CAMPS

Sat. March 25
At 6.30 we left by lorry for El-Shatt [Yugoslav Refugee camp]. Dropped people and baggage at Camp 1 and came straight on, 4 of us, to Camp 2, where we met Major Bekker, i/c and some of his officers, South Africans. My job will be to take charge of half the welfare work... we sleep in one large tent, Charles throwing his weight about in small matter of reserving a corner for himself!

Mon. 27
Checking mistakes in original registrations. Lots of enquiries during day and there were times when as many as four languages were being cross-talked in the 'office' ... The Arabs were dismissed with an hour's notice today by Bekker. (Filthy treatment of Arabs — no wonder they act as they do. How can they trust us?)

Tues. 28
Wallet has disappeared (containing all my money, about £9). Police conducted a perfunctory examination and a rather gross parade of Arab work people, one of whom was carrying a little hashish. (What a brutish way we treat these people.) ...I have never before seen an executive office in a worse shambles than this Camp HQ.

Fri. 31
The afternoon was completely taken up with a shambles over the vaccination arrangements for tomorrow. The inoculation tent has been taken over by a group from a tent that is being tiled, and they won't move (reasonably enough — sitting a couple of days and nights in the desert is no joke, especially for people who left Dalmatia on the Allied promise of houses in Italy), though the Major stupidly ordered them to.

Mon. April 3

…all the army people here bitter against the 'black animals', wanting to go down to their village and 'smoke them out', 'shoot them up'. Ready to kill off the 'wogs'. T.T. rampaging against them and their paganism, their filth, their gross ingratitude for the white man's favours …South Africans had drinking session as prelude to a Suez dinner party in the mess, and behaved like animals, a favourite game being 'belly-shoving' (their figures are built for this).

Thurs. 6

Major takes exception to my German grammar, swearing that he wouldn't have 'this bloody language in my bloody camp'. …Sports Committee persuaded to help get deck tennis, rounders and quoits under way, and also put in a little work on the football pitch-to-be. …(It is Maundy Thursday) — The procession began at 9 pm. At each kitchen an altar had been set up, and in the church, the small poor altar had been improved by the addition of white altar cloths, a red cloth and front curtains, candles and oil lamps. Five villages each make up their own procession, starting at the church and the four kitchens. Headed by glowing lamp-bearers and a crucifix draped in black, they moved slowly round from altar to altar. The crucifix bearer was barefoot or in socks only. At each altar the torches grouped round the altar whilst an elderly man mournfully sang a slow, sad dirge, in half tones, rising and falling interminably. Then Pater Nosters and Ave Marias were chanted, briskly, liltingly, and the procession moved on to visit and walk round the next 'chapel' before entering and repeating the ceremony. In Yugo-S this starts much later at night and goes on until daybreak … I felt at one with them all, despite all the physical difficulties, including, I'm ashamed to say, that of the unwashed smell. (But whose fault? They have water at the few stand-pipes only a couple of times a day, and they queue for the small amount they can get for washing, laundry, cooking).

Tues. 11

Bekker issued instructions for a permanent transfer of personnel to Camp 3 in the morning. No consultation with unit leader as laid down …when position as agreed by the authorities concerned put to him, he swore and blinded and raised Cain "Mutiny, bloody mutiny!" This camp is hopelessly chaotic, unorganised. Delvin's expression is 'I'm disgusted". Middle East Relief & Rehabilitation Agency is to be UNRRA as from May 1.

Fri. 14

Went into every tent in Block C to encourage people into the lorries for the bathhouse and then disinfestation. Lice run round the collars like tiny cars on a busy highway; we work in clouds of DDT, protests, fleas and lice. Then registration …interminable …visit of HS of Friends Service Council prompted comparison with many UNRRA officials who are simply careerists, and South Africans who can only rave at natives, and boast of their own prowess.

POLITICAL MANIPULATION – PEASANT ROOTS

Tues. 25

"We are evacuees, allied evacuees. Here there is no wire because there is desert. In other camps there is wire because they are POWs. But here there is no wire, only desert." How many refugees feel like this, feel they are being treated simply as prisoners with only the most basic of needs catered for, and then most inadequately? Dysentery everywhere, the whole hygiene set-up falling down on the job. Many not turned up yet for inoculation. Asked Gorpacic about my feeling that there was underground pressure making people afraid to be open. He admitted all camps riddled with 'informers', 'secret police', some kind of Communist agents who have a lot of power — yet great number of these people (Dalmatians) were not Partisans, and he added that the committees on which we tend to rely were not in any way representative. Who thought up this whole scheme — or was it thought? …several references to promise that El-Shatt would be 'land of milk and honey'.

Sun 14 May

Staff is to work 24 hours, 7 day week, says Major. …Evening, struggled along to children's concert, the only notable points being the lovely national dance and song in national costume by about 15 little girls, dressed in red with long white socks, and the small boy who stood in front of the choir, cross-eyed, and picked his nose.

Wed. 17

It is not good for a sad heart to listen to Y-S singing. It makes it still sadder. Branko was singing 'Madeline' today with that sad, plaintive style which is quite hypnotic. Hypnotic — no wonder they love to sing.

DOUBTS, FRUSTRATIONS, FOREBODINGS

Thurs. 2 June

Following more refugee arrivals I was off (hitching) to Palestine on a course (H&S), then back to El-Shatt on 21st. I wondered what we had done since we came out to justify the efforts which have been put into equipping and supplying us. There were rumours of a move back to Cairo preparatory to a move into the Balkans. Time drags on. An article (illustrated) in Picture Post, shows ATS [Auxiliary Territorial Service, later Women's Royal Army corps] in Italy, refugee girl driver, etc. Photo actually taken in Mena, refugee girl was Susie Yellin who has never been a refugee. Article all to hell. ATS Company has never left Egypt. What can one believe?

It wasn't until Wed. 29 November that we sailed — from Alexandria

BOUND FOR GREECE

Sat. 2 Dec

Hove to in Port Said — bullion going aboard in boxes. Said to be seven and a half million pounds worth and the captain thinks it's nickel. He is a splendid character from Aughton Park, typical Liverpudlian. Aged 64, has been in 3 wars and in this had lost 2 ships under him, the last one blowing up some 14 months ago.

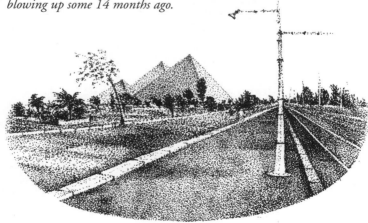

The Mena Straight

At Coptic Monastery, Wadi Natrum

Sun. 3

By 11 o'clock our pilot boarded us and slowly we moved off. De Lesseps statue, insignificant and poorly shaped, passed us. Out at sea we ran into the edge of a storm which leaves biggish rollers. Hitting us beam on, the smallest rollers have had their effect, Cecil, Gerald, Roy, Harry, Mike, Hubert all having to lie down. I think the weather is delightful, keen and sharp, warm when you get into a sheltered corner, it's bringing back all the life which seemed to stultify in Egypt, and is sweeping away the sultry deadness of that land.

Fri.. 8 Dec.

Churchill wins vote of confidence over allegation that British troops are being used to bolster up reactionary regimes in Belgium, Holland, Italy and Greece, with particular reference to Greece. …we watch planes diving out of a grey sky to bomb and cannon the guerilla elements. Fierce bombardments were taken for thunder rolling over the city, they were so heavy. How much longer shall we be here? We seem to be further from our landing day than ever. It's over a fortnight since we left Alex and stronger than ever is the frustration of the months we've been out so far and the little we've achieved. Does London (Leeds) know? Now we're within swimming distance and the guns on shore are popping, wounded men from the docks are brought on to the nearby hospital ship. Food is said to be short, the main bridge on the Pir-Athens road has been blown … warships in Salamis Bay joined in by dropping some big stuff on Partisan strongholds.

Wed. 13

Moved 2 or 3 miles west into the bay nearer Piraeus. Harry and Roy delivered safely by Capt. Hope at about 11 am … in Athens there is no food, no light, no heat, shops closed, little water. ELAS [pro-communist partisans] have the range of ML HQ and are dropping shells on the roof, there is constant sniping and 3-cornered battles. Dead bodies often lie a long time before burial. (John Dula has been picking up bodies and burying them).

GREECE

Sun. 24 December, 1944

After so many delays and false starts, managed to land with first truck load and stay ashore. None of ours came ashore but there were 3 unaccompanied Humbers. Bullets straying about: humming like steady flights of bees above our heads made place where transport parked rather uncomfortable. Some more trucks damaged. Pot-holed road led from docks to main road, lined with broken, dead houses, and few figures that moved were like shadows. Freezing. Snow on mountains.

Tues. 26

Certain difficulties (to do with IVSP moving) owing to our wanting to offload in house opposite the conference place. (Chu'll & Eden attend conference to which ELAS delegates have been invited.) Earlier had seen Humbler 8 cwt still on quay, so decided to 'borrow' it. A heart-stopping breakdown almost opposite slogan-plastered Brewery from which mortars are frequently lobbed on and over the road.

POLITICS V HUMANITY

Sun. 31

Lazarus and I were on call and emergency evacuation of hospital in ELAS hands came in shortly after return from Mass in Cathedral. ... Two 3-tonners and two 15 cwt were draped with Stars and Stripes — much to Wallberg's disgust, and our indignation.
(UNRRA, in the popular view, is taking on a purely American character and Military Liaison are sore at the accent placed on the USA aspect of relief.) At about 2 pm we passed the barriers into ELAS territory. We had

two hours in which to work. Hooting and moving slowly, we reached the hospital. There was sniping all about. We had difficulty in getting them to open the doors to us; then we entered and the parleying began. Time passed and no agreement seemed imminent. Many things stand out — the tall girl and the short one, both snipers, dressed in blouse and trousers, with bandoliers and rifles, and red scarves thrown round their necks. Very striking girls. The mixture of unhappy patients, tired, worn doctors and nurses (the nurse with big brown eyes who spoke good English and the one who cried when they brought in the four-year-old kiddie shot in the leg); the strutting, conceited young fellows, the man whose leg had been amputated and the one who was screaming in pain; the old lady from Norfolk reading the life of Henry VII, the French speaking couple who were so charming, the young partisans singing ELAS songs as they leaned on their guns. Parleying going on and on, then we began to move the patients down, making them as comfortable as possible in the cramped room in the trucks. Then there were the awful minutes when the order came to take back into the wards all those we had just evacuated. The tanks were in position down the road and across from the hospital. The minute hand was hovering on the brink of 4 o'clock and we had to depart in haste. There were tears in my eyes. The tanks will — 'will' if the army plan is carried out — open fire into the doorway and then blow the hospital and all those people to pieces before morning. The aged, the sick and wounded, those whose smile had made us so welcome, whether partisan or not... Later we ratified the decision not to work under the mantle of the Stars and Stripes.

Mon. January 1
There was a big fire consuming houses in the area of the hospital we tried to evacuate yesterday I was in utter misery.

Wed. 3
The hospital, not 'liberated', was evacuated today. The doorway had been shelled, but the defenders surrendered and no lives of patients or staff were lost. Immensely relieved.

Sun. 7
Helping at hospital. They certainly made me very welcome and I was stuffed with boiled rice and bully. Helped carry wounded to hospital, then

took staff to various homes down sharp, broken, rocky side streets in which I got lost. Driving almost blind — shots across the front of the truck pulled me up. Warned I was running into ELAS band 2 km down the road.

ON TO THESSALY

Tues. Feb. 6
With Willi surveyed Nea Arikhialos, a miserable sight. What was once a fair, flourishing settlement (refugees from Bulgaria) now a debris of 800 destroyed homes out of 850. Sugar £2 an och. Medicines short, scabies is widespread, there is need for clothing. Italians even destroyed school.

Thurs. 8
Mail came up with Walt whose coat, overalls and shaving equipment were kleftied from the truck whilst he was up and down the stairs. We've lost 2 spare wheels and sundry cans of petrol during the last few days.

Fri/Sat. 16/17
To Elasson from Larissa across the moors. Dora nearly shot. from Elasson to recce Tsaritsani. These recces essential, though time-consuming, and I have to wonder (uncharitably?) if information is entirely accurate. But no doubt about need. Road full of enormous pot-holes which get Willi riled.

Mar. 1/2
Work on trucks; contact REME for spares. Trucks take a terrible bashing on bad roads and often too heavy loads. Shackle pins, springs, petrol systems. Blanketing stolen — 5 National Guards billeted on us for safeguard! Not again!!

Tues. March 6
In evening took the 3 tonner and with Arthur carried a month's supply of milk supplies for 500 children to Tsaritsani. Inspected place proposed for use as milk centre, and also soup kitchen, a pitiful sight where, in a bare, thin board shack, 100 children feed every day on beans and water.

Wed. 7
Indoors working out some of the questions I wanted the Central Committee International Red Cross to answer, and also some other odd questions which

occurred to me that needed answering by someone. So much flour, so much milk still to come to complete the 3000 rations; the Central Committee to see; the hospital to visit; the milk centre to be given a quick visit ...and my day ended with map referencing of villages I'm now responsible for and checking in the remainder of the milk I was expecting.

ROAD IMPASSABLE

Sat 10

To Valanida the road was pretty dangerous, narrow and strewn with sharp stones — twists & turns & sudden sharp ascents and descents from one road to the other all the way. Found here that EA district Committee was prepared to receive the food, having been warned by Elasson that we would be soon delivering in their area. But we handed over to the old IRC committee, just in case and inserted their names on the list. (Everywhere one finds evidence of the failings of the Elasson Central Committee. Politics.) Pushed on along an even worse road to Krania, where we made a recce sitting in the sun outside the village 'shop' surrounded by hundreds of the locals. Specimens of local bread produced, also local food, wild vegetables and herbs, maize and rye but without sufficient salt to taste it. A still worse road towards Dheskati. On the hill out of Krania we stopped for yoghourt, egg and bread, a tasty meal. There was a wonderful view down the broad valley and over towards the broad white head and shoulders of Olympus. We didn't reach Dheskati. The incredible road, which we almost lost more than once, forded rivers at their deepest reaches, and dived and twisted with sheer ferocity. Snow appeared on the road and we were soon cutting through quite a lot of drifts. Then we stuck on a fat wedge of snow, with deep muddy ruts underneath. We dug our way out after 20 minutes and carried on only to stick again higher up.... Sadly we managed to turn round almost bogging down again in the mud, and came back, one tyre badly cut by the chains.

DESTITUTION

There was no soup kitchen or milk centre in Valanida, but we discussed where both could be provided and there was firm promise. 30 days rations of sugar, milk, flour and soup for the 224 children under 8 (out of pop.

of 725) to start with. Whole village undernourished. Has never been self-sufficient in food — people mainly shepherds — and since it lost 20 of its 45 pair of oxen to the Germans, it has managed to sow only half the fields. No stocks of food, and flour, salt, rice, pulses and sugar are badly needed, and fuel. About half their sheep and goats were taken by the Germans. Clothing is as desperate a need as food. Malaria affects the whole population, and they have a stock of 2000 quinine tablets, and no other medicines. No doctor. No certificated midwife. 30 homes completely burnt out of 130. Timber needed to repair school and make desks, benches etc. As Gov. teacher was not paid, he returned home. No soap.

Sun. 11

On to Likoudi via 3 diversions because of broken bridges. Wonderful characters at Likoudi; good store. Against many of the burnt houses, wood, branch and straw shelters have been erected for the families of the destroyed houses.... At Gerania, lying in lovely rolling country under the shining white of Olympus facing over towards black rugged mountains, we found conditions worse ... In 1943 their whole stock of wheat and corn was burnt, and in 1944 they were forced to work by night only, which resulted in their sowing very little. The locust plague on top of this reduced their crops to only one month's supply of food. Pre-war they sowed 3500 stremata; this year 300. Draught animals reduced from 75-80 pair of oxen to 13 pair mixed oxen and mules. Now they have no cows (pre-war 300) and only 800 sheep (pre-war 3500). Came away from the crowds of ragged people and ragged, cold children (many dressed in remnants of traditional clothing) with clapping and Jivios. Amazing resilience. On the way back, handed over Micro Eleftohori's food. Back home, still feeling sick, tho' I've existed on half a dish of yoghourt today, to beans, bully and potatoes fried en masse, and the dim cold of my room.

Tues. 13

The track to Olympia and Kalivia Kokkinoplos led out of Kalithea across the meadows, straight towards the wonderful snow mass of Olympus. It could have been a lovely trip but unfortunately the track rapidly deteriorated and, with a substantial load in the truck, became quite dangerous. In one narrow deep gully we both stuck and lost a front right shackle pin. My temper was fraying and it was getting later and later. I'd eaten nothing since morning. Jacked up the truck in the gully, having *first to unload part of supplies, and eventually got the pin back part way. Went on, the narrow track winding above a sheer drop and only inches to spare (centimetres!) and reached Olymbia about 6.15, worn and weary. Everyone waiting. Kalivia's mules came running across when they saw us! Unloaded, insisted on Olymbia wiping off the KKE (Communist Party) slogans scrawled all over the truck, and, the prospect of a wretched night return trip to Kalithea lending bias to the decision, finally accepted the offer of a bed for the night in Olymbia. But first, before even being able to find a corner from the crowds in which to eat, had to go over to the neighbouring village of Flamboura, where I listed some of their needs. The headlamps blazed the trail back to my bed and the stove in the room lit up a circle of more questioning, talking faces. At about 10 we ate eggs and bread and a form of pastry (soft, damp, more like a pancake). Another village had come in, and there was more questioning. I pulled the thick woollen blanket over me, kicked off my boots, the family did the same on the other side of the stove, and silence came down at last.*

Mar. 29

Still feeling very sick. … Politics is a sickness here, and a deathly one. … Something before 6 I took my first walk up the hill for over a fortnight. It was lovely. I lay with my nose to the sweet earth, speckled with tiny blue flowers. I watched the young hawks in the sky. I felt the soft firm earth beneath me and looked up to watch the clouds overhead. It was like reaching back into the past. I tried to empty my mind of the confusing, whirligig things, and let it reabsorb the strength and happiness of the earth. The storks have come home again to the church. I could see their whiteness against the brown as clearly as I could see the white cross around which they have their nest.

HEADACHES FROM BRICK WALLS

Sat. 7 April

Committee meeting developed which was so completely unsatisfactory that at one point I quite lost my temper … rowed them about yesterday's visits, drafted a letter to the villages, explained again what action is necessary on D43 (Requisition form), told them again their ruddy lists were no bloody good, tore my hair, and subsided. Went out to watch them giving chick peas, pieces of bread and dry fish to 518 school children

The storks have come home again to the church

in Elasson school ... but was interrupted by arrival of bran and poison for locusts. Found warehouse for it. Home to eat and write reports. Now, shall I, at 10.30, go to the dance for 'ELAS soldiers', or not? I know it won't be a dance, but they've borrowed a side bulb from my truck.

RIDERS ON THE GRAVY TRAIN

Wed 11
Came down to Dolikhi and up to Ayios Dimitrios to pick up timber for houses in Pazalades. Locust hoppers like dark snow. I look back and see tyre tracks crushed into the moving mass. Something must be done.

Thurs. 12
Cecil in bed. To UNRRA office to see Agricultural Adviser/Expert. I was shocked, to put it mildly. The big Texan official, well-fed, well-groomed, lay back in his armchair with his cowboy boots up on the desk, smoke curling up from a cigar in an ashtray. I presented him with my cigarette tins, packed with hoppers, and sketched the position and the need. His

reply was that no-one would get him to go up 'that' road again - unless maybe in the event of their making a decent road. The fact that locusts were starving the people made no impact. This fellow - and the chief of mission who buys Greek gold to convert into UNRRA badges that he can send home to circumvent currency restrictions - these are the people manning what I remember Max Melling in a letter I had in Egypt called 'the hope of the world': UNRRA. I haven't met a decent UNRRA man yet.

SELF-HELP? - WELL ...

Tues. 17

(In Larissa) spent an hour with the Nomarch going over D3 with a fine toothcomb, trying to talk sweet reasonableness into him. What an incredible man to be in a position of responsibility for people. ... Collected petrol and half Elasson (15 people) and made tired way home. Just outside Elasson, a mile or so, burst a rear tyre. collected help from an Army unit camped 3 or 4 miles back, changed wheels, drove into Elasson, returned the wheel and left the truck jacked up in as good a position as possible. At the suggestion of unloading the 2000 ocques I carried, the gathered populace faded softly away into the night. I bedded down by midnight.

Wed. 18

Long arguments with the Mayor, President D3 and villages, and I think I made them accept that they have to revise their attitude somewhat, Nomarch or no Nomarch. Disappointment at finding that Electric Coy, after I've spent so much time ensuring that they get oil, have done nothing to repair the lines, and starting today will take 10 days over the job whilst the oil lies in their warehouse.

Fri. 27

In clothing store, where the committee's gloating eyes assured me of their intention to rob the store of some of the best articles. What a blessing it would be to have one or two extra people here. One alone is forced to hop about from one thing to another and try to be another Argus.

Mon. May 7

In Volos. Took family from down below up into hills, through Portaria and finally over the top until we were looking down on the gulf of Salonika, and could see Mount Athos. Dora and Willi left their truck by the side of the road whilst they sought other occupation than guarding it. We were back when the MPs brought Willi's truck down. John R. went out to rescue the stranded D&W.

CONFUSION FOREBODING AND FRUSTRATION

Fri. 11

Took Cecil to REME re his truck. Both of us felt a bit grim about things. Confusion over position and future. UNRRA and VS work and replacements ... Back in Elasson, visited man beaten up a few days ago, got Anagnostoulis out of gaol for a few minutes (he wasn't in a fit state to take any part in proceedings). Some nasty moments — but must let National Guard & prison authorities know that claims of ill-treatment are noticed by outsiders. Position not improved by trouble over Easter, including the beating up of the N.G. corporal by British troops and his carting off to Kozani or Salonika.

Sun. 27

Back to Elasson at about midday, packed up clothing for Domenico and spent until 8.15 giving it out. Quite reasonable at first, there were difficult moments, and as at Kalithea there was chaos at the end. Whole thing needs rethinking. Held up for 20 minutes re my spare wheel by the Nat. Guard who threatened to shoot me. Retained spare wheel.

Sat. June 2

Certain difficulties at Tirnavos and I realise how little of what I should I put on paper. In Elasson everything quite haywire. I am mad, and am rude, refusing at first to drink coffee with these 'letter'-bound bureaucrats.

Fri. July 27

Brought up some basic supplies from Volos for children's camps.

Sat. 28

Meet the group who are interested in children's camps and tell them what I've already arranged. See Gymnasium schoolmaster and tell him about school supplies and get him in on camps. Arrange to see school tomorrow.

Sun 29

I met the committee I agreed to put in charge of the holiday camp project, and we went thoroughly into all the details with fairly satisfactory results and committed volunteers.

Sat. 18 Aug.

D&I set out for Stormion and the kids at Kokkino Nero ... found that no caique sailing that night. Eventually settled down on beach and ate bread and cheese. Then inside nets to read a while with the aid of inspection lamp. Sleep to the murmur of the sea. Arriving at K.N. most embarrassing, but delightful to see the little brats so happy. Have to greet them all. Walk up river bed where water still comes down stained with iron. Drank from a leaf spout and hurried down to beach where caique back and ready for return. D. lost her bedroll on drive back to Larissa.

Fri. 24th

Up at 5.30 ... several tearful last-minute entreaties by children not on list, led to my increasing the number to 75 ... in Stormion, caique man wants not only half an ocean of kerosene but my skid and snow chains as well. Jams, fruit, ovaltines, medicines, football etc. to Kokkino Nero, and back to Larissa.

Wed. Sept 5

Off to Olymbias where Karia mules waiting. Transferred loads to mules and put truck near Vice-Pres's house. Mount my mule. Pleasant ride for a couple of hours though I had to close my eyes to the sheer drops below my, thankfully, sure footed animal. Then the rains came. 12 cows and an unknown number of sheep said to have been killed by hailstones in Karia. Thought I should die of cold, frozen to my little mule. Arriving about 9.30, I saw the clothing safely deposited, and wondered, in view of the persistent rumours of theft by committee members, what sort of hand had been made of this lot; Not a very comfortable night.

Fri. 7

An early start after night when Pres. barricaded house against feared attack. I enjoyed the mule-cum-shanks pony trip over the hills to Olymbia. Sun and dappled shade across the wooded hills, saw no sign of the dreaded boars but found group of charcoal burners busy with their dome-shaped, mud-plastered 'converter'.

Mon. 4 Feb. 1946
Morning spent discussing child Welfare & D43. This followed by lunch and a discussion on one or two points raised with Derek Edwards and Godfrey Heaven (who arrived last night).

Wed. 6
Had promised Derek a clothing distribution so went down to office and arranged that clothing be ready by midday. Dora, Ethelwyn & Godfrey went off to Farsala. Eventually got into Dhassohori. The distribution did not go as well as it might have done, but I suppose not too badly. (Nothing like the distribution at Athanata last December when the lists had been cooked by a small right wing clique, and where the Pres had been attacked and might have had it had I not interfered quickly.) With Simos reading out the names and bundle numbers, things were just a trifle slow, and there was some trouble over the President's having been put down to receive 7 bundles for a family of 9! And it appears that he has a considerable number of sheep and was probably undeserving of even one bundle. Such wonderful people up here in the mountains, but always there are those who have (by one means or another) amassed more than others, get a taste of power, are frequently associated with the royalist or right wing, and see a gap between them and their fellows. The bitter split between Left and Right is shame enough, splitting as it does communities and families. We had a spot more bother at the end (where the poorer parcels have a habit of gathering) and then ate K rations, supplemented by cheese and bread, in the house of a very decent sort of man who spoke a little English.

MISSION ACCOMPLISHED?

Mon. Feb. 11
[IVSP] meeting. My idea of going home via Switzerland seems rather remote. Some idea of people's vague notions for the future came out — and how vague. Anyway we pack up at the end of March, and by the end of April we shall all be sitting in Athens waiting for the 'off'. How long will it be, I wonder, before I want to be back in Greece — seeing only the beauties, the delights, the friendliness, the sunshine. Much depends, I suppose, on whether I can settle down in England. If I can't, I shall be infernally miserable. There's nothing for me there.

Tues. April 23
Off to Athens

Thurs. May 2
Saw The Idiot in Greek, with Thea, Eleni and the unit. Very well produced and acted, and an appropriate way of spending our last evening in Greece. Our last evening in London was spent at the theatre.

SNAPSHOTS, GREECE

Ethelwyn Best (Unit 1)

The thousands of hostages taken by ELAS (Communists) in the civil was who wanted little else but to get home again. Often, though seriously ill, they preferred a blanket on the floor of an empty warehouse to a bed in a hospital in case they should miss a chance of a place in a truck, or a caique if they were island folk.

An awkward problem of a group of about 65 refugees, with dogs, cats, chickens, turkeys, goats, a pig and two fine oxen as well as the fruits of their year's farming, which had to be sent home to a village near the Bulgarian border. They were got off — some by caique, the rest, including the animals, but 3-ton truck by road.

Never enough of the right sort of second-hand clothing; but it was rewarding too — one will never forget the small boy who slept with his new shoes under his pillow, or the other who kissed them before putting them on.

The warm response to the fact that the team were volunteers and the interest they took in individual problems, even when material help was not available; and the resulting encouragement to tackle jobs the local people might have felt beyond them if working alone.

The handicap to the voluntary workers to be tied to a large organisation [UNRRA] working primarily at official levels and often unaware of actual conditions in the field, or unable, through its own constitution, to take any direct action to deal with them.

The GREEK VENTURE
early 1945

Godfrey Heaven
Senior Representative

TAKING THE REINS

One COBSRA party was shipped to Greece, and promptly back again, as ELAS, the communist-led army of EAM (the coalition of the left) that dominated most of Greece was threatening Athens. Churchill intervened, turning civil strife and terror into war, and an indefinite delay for us. I attended my first COBSRA meeting, and consultations with other societies, and Military Liaison at their HQ, but mainly in our COBSRA office, a room in the Save the Children Fund one, staffed by a volunteer of theirs with phone and typewriter. The Red Cross also had their own office.

UNRRA appointed a stolid, mid-western senator as voluntary societies liaison officer, totally ignorant of either our or UNRRA's procedures, so that half of his work seemed to be signing letters I had written. As for accounts, he had never heard of £.s.d and was unable to cope with divisions of twelve. I suggested our typist (and interpreter as needed) could deal with that. And with most of my work, I thought, feeling under-extended!

I was surprised what little contact the welfare staff had with the people: not even their alphabet. Heard a couple mention Posybeat street: the name, I said, was Roosevelt, renamed in their honour. They would waste time waiting for the UNRRA taxi to their hotel, ignorant of the tram to it every few minutes, a simple indicator and phrase for the trivial fare. Conductors wouldn't collect from us in khaki: Churchill will pay, they'd say.

I knew from Willi's reports of the problems of distribution

to local committees, supplies getting to one faction only, or being sold. We decided my best plan was to visit the worker in each centre: had a unit meeting so they were expecting me.

FIELD NOTES

LARISSA, Beryl Verling-Brown's centre, had a relatively good local committee. Next day a bus to TRIKKALA, Dora Tregenza's, and slept in the welcoming house where she lodged. A very unsettled area: I had previously been recommended to go to see the head of Aries Velouchiotis, a forceful and treacherous ELAS leader, impaled on a pole in the market square. The little town had suffered: few facilities, church precincts and alleyways soiled by the excreta of those not caring to walk out to a field or grove. Burnt ruins of houses, starved children. Neighbouring KALAMBAKA was more seriously ravaged. Dora, and Roy Richards who was there *pro tem*, ably in charge. Sunday I walked with Roy up the spiral track to the ruined Meteora Monastery - rather scared to see the shapes of men with guns peering down. No sign of them on top, probably poor refugees with sticks, hiding, scared of us.

CRETE

Khaniá

CRETE Iráklion

CRETE. I stayed with Derek Maunder at his pleasant lodgings in Khania.   The island was settling down, and local people, one hopes, would take on the job the team had seen through here, so now it was only who goes where. In fact there would be only four to join me staying here. I was able to visit a mountain camp the team had run, near the ancient Venetian-Turkish capital of Iraklion, and tour the remoter east and south of the island. Also to walk out and see the family of a girl I met by chance on the ship. She had been involved with a German during the occupation, had suffered for it since - her hair had not yet fully grown. She had his unit address and begged me to write, having no idea of the danger, even if he survived the retreat. To see her family, then, and introduced to her brother who had a taverna in Khania, as a means of contact if I could.   They were peasants with a bit of vine and olive just outside the town, who received me gladly. I explained I understood how the brave guerillas in the mountains felt about her affaire, but urged that both of them were young and ignorant of all that went before, and he was obeying orders; that with peace must come forgiveness for the younger generation - and for the sake of the family - or we shall have continuous bloody war.

Then another brother of the one who kept the Taverna (where I ate), offered me a flight in a stripped-down Vulcan of his, a regular trade. We had a final meal. They agreed with my contention. "We beat the bastards so now it's all over!" She thanked me, but wept as I said she could only wait for peace. I felt I'd done some good, as much in being the strange 'anglo' as for my equally strange speech.

ALARMS AND EXCURSIONS

It was an alarming flight. Up from the airstrip close to the waves, a piece flew off and we circled back to what felt like a crash landing. Only engine cowling, so off again, just clearing the water, to land on the strip by dark in Athens, closed and without lights - and would I help unload? It was drums of smuggled olive oil, a portent of trade getting back to normal!

RANDOM JOTTINGS

Derek Maunder (Unit 2)

There was a considerable delay in our being called forward and for some of the time we were deployed in the refugee camps in Egypt. I spent a period working in the Greek camp at Moses Wells and others went to the Yugoslav camp at El Shatt. Later some of us served on transit camps looking after Jewish people from the Yemen on their way to Palestine - I cannot remember why this particular movement took place at that point since the Yemen was not a war zone. A particular job was de-lousing which involved puffing clouds of DDT over people in the belief that it was very good for them. In fact, we presumably absorbed more than the patients.

It finally became clear that we were not going to Yugoslavia and about the time of the German surrender we were called forward and allocated to Crete. At that time Military Liaison was still responsible for civil relief but UNRRA was in the process of taking over and we became part of what was to be Region K. The food situation in general was not desperate but virtually everything else was in very short supply or non-existent. A typical example was spares for vehicles: tyres and most other parts were virtually unobtainable, at least on the open market. Our transport park had to be specially guarded each night, but even so, the policeman on duty was found one morning asleep in a truck, jacked up, with the wheels removed.

3/6/45

The gravest problem in Crete is that of apathy - unlike the pre-war Crete when the people were, I am told, if anything over-enterprising. We can hope that whatever we do here, in the right spirit, will go towards rebuilding the island in a larger sense.

18/6/45

Somebody said to me today: "Thank goodness they've sent us a team that doesn't mind roughing it."

The worst hit were those in the destroyed villages - villages in which all buildings had been systematically dynamited usually in response to guerilla activity in the location. For example, every village through which Kreipe (the kidnapped German C-in-C) had passed *en route* to the south coast for a rendezvous with a submarine taking him to Egypt, had been destroyed. An early task was to construct an index of such cases so that help could be given quickly to those living in misery among the ruins of their homes.

27/7/45

40 villages have been razed in Crete. If only we could begin on even one village, rebuilding the school. Villagers would be able to use it as emergency shelter over the coming winter. Every week is vital as we are now coming to the end of July and have only till the end of October. It is the most important contribution we can make to the welfare of the island. When you have gone round and talked to the villagers, you feel no task is more worthwhile. We would be giving them something they would certainly not have at all but for our efforts. As a team we could tackle the job, independent of other often unreliable organisations.

We did initiate a major project of felling to provide timber for re-building. The source was a burnt forest at a village in the eastern part of the island called Prina and it had the merit of not destroying scarce living trees. Our role in this was primarily encouragement and co-ordination. Another major team activity was investigating and trying to meet the needs of orphanages. They were short of practically everything and regular supplies of food, blankets and clothing were organized.

27/7/45

Beatrice, Bob and Huw are in charge, sorting the clothing, coping valiantly with a gang of between 20 and 30 excited women. The clothing is in a pretty filthy state and a lot of it in rags - not a very pleasant job. But it is not only clothing - the other day Bob discovered a bag with four live bombs in it, which he promptly had dropped over the quay-side into the sea.

One of the first jobs for some members of the unit was the sorting of captured supplies that could be used for civilian purposes.

27/7/45

Margaret has collected from Khania a load of salvage for use in re-starting home industries. She will start craft instruction in orphanages. [cf Schleswig pp 159-60]
At Iraklion the remainder of us have succeeded against all odds in getting the children's camp at Daphnais open.

As these examples suggest, the team was never involved in the kind of life and death situation for which we had been trained and we found ourselves carrying out a variety of mildly useful roles but without any integrated team function and indeed without any very clearly defined responsibilities. In the autumn some team members were moved to Greece and by the following January the team was finally disbanded.

CRETE & GREECE

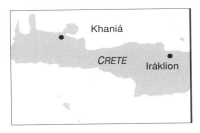

RRU 13 (Unit 2)
Reuben Say (Unit 2)

Initially we were based on Iraklion in Crete.   One of our responsibilities was Neapolis Orphanage on which I reported favourably, considering the circumstances, on 30th November 1945. Evidently, supplies, such as they were, had to be channelled through the local authorities, and sadly, many old scores related to collaboration, and distrust between political groups, were only just surfacing;   so the fairness of distribution of aid was often suspect.

When the Unit was transferred to mainland Greece, I was assigned to the islands of Cephalonia and Ithaca.   In the light of my experiences there, the orphanage I reported on in Crete seemed unusually fortunate.   I remember an orphanage on Cephalonia in really desperate trouble - open to the skies in many places, the children almost starving, while monies were available which could only be touched by obtaining the signature of a local "worthy" who dared not return to the island as he had collaborated with the Nazis. I shall never be quite free of a desperately sad memory of Davrata, a small village which had been chosen by the SS for a reprisal, like Lidice in Poland. It was solely inhabited by grieving widows and orphans; every house in the village had been gutted and de-roofed, and the tragic little band of widows took me to see the blood-stained rocks where all their men-folk had been shot.

Against this, I set my happy and privileged memory of being taken by the local schoolmaster on Ithaca, to help him unearth the archaeological treasures, buried before the invasion, including some supposedly associated with Ulysses.   To this period also belongs my most embarrassing memory, when a nurse from the USA and myself, being the first non-Germans on the island, were a focus for an outpouring of joy at liberation. We had to 'run the gauntlet' as we walked to church in Argostolion, with what appeared to be the entire population lining a long road, and cheering madly, while they rang the church bells. I felt a most awful phony!

My overall feelings were of inadequacy and frustration, with such an enormous task and little that could be done except send off appeals to Athens. However, as most relief workers in Greece found, the friendliness of the Greek people, and their courage in adversity, gave me memories which I shall always treasure.

TIGHTENING-UP THE SYSTEM

Godfrey Heaven

PATRAS. I met the regional director. ex-ML Colonel, still very much a colonel, though a gentle man. First asked to deal with immediate problems: they just dealt with each applicant at the warehouse till the consignment was finished. I went with a girl from the office to interpret: asked one applicant for shoes where she came from. Then where did you wash your feet? I asked in Greek (the roads were snow and slush). Consternation. So in future it had to be a chit from the office, and if the applicant appeared not to be in dire need it had to be a firm 'no', there was not enough to go round. The KED (central distribution committee) seemed to be working well - all stores under the sharp eye of a Greek staff member who'd been in business in Chicago, and didn't give a damn for local factions. Only sugar and flour this month.

COLLEAGUES AND VICTIMS

To KALAVRITA, at the request of Helen Graham (Girl Guides). The Germans, in a reprisal raid, had taken all the men of the little town and shot them, locked the women in the church and set it on fire. Most managed to escape: the clock still stands at 2.43. She drove the truck up the serpentine mountain road to their camp, a double tent for the two of them; my bedroll in a store tent. I noted a few matters to investigate but it was evident they were coping well, a dedicated work for peace. Walked up the street. A woman with young daughter gave me some account of their sorrows, and I felt I'd merely be swanning to go any further. I'll never forget what I'd seen of the emaciated survivors in scanty shelters, with small, smoky fires outside, among snowy ruins. I returned on the UNRRA truck. One request promptly fulfilled, that trucks should take people only with our permission, and only those with relatives or a specific need. Speculative solicitors had been there.

AITOLIA-AKARNANIA, Feb - April, 1945. Made my base at Agrinion, in the hotel: minimal but fairly clean and friendly, and the little room off the pavement I could use. A lamb put its head in and bleated. In addition to our and the other Volsoc workers, there was Nancy, a welfare worker running children's camps and Nel, Red Cross nurse, both American, directly under UNRRA, though I saw them more often than ours. They and I had jeeps, the others small trucks, with drivers always to be in charge - too many wheels or whole vehicles had been lost when parked. I, at least, was delighted to have my own chauffeur, others less so.

He was Solon, an honest, simple man, excellent on these earthen, rocky roads. Coming at fair speed first time to cross the Bailey bridge that replaces the ruined one over the Acheloos, I called Stop! He did, so quickly the girders rattled. Didn't you see that big sign? We backed slowly. "Ah, for letters my eyes are ..." I asked him not to be ashamed of being unable to read: his folk had had no chance: he's a much better driver, and I can do the reading if he stops. I'd seen the word danger, and read out that the bridge would not bear wheeled vehicles. We had a long detour, adjusting stones, across the river in spate. He told me he had fought in ELAS, had his home burnt, mother and sister killed: he was desperately hoping now to be safe with wife and son in

Patras. I explained how we worked - against all war and not in politics. so that hungry people could live - yet he had my sympathy. Also that he could talk to me freely and I would not pass on his remarks. It proved very useful later.

Here there were a few small villages in the hills. Nel had got some children's milk service going where there were schools, but there was a corrupt general distribution. Two said they sold the stuff: most people could pay for it. The logic that if they could pay, they are the ones that shouldn't get it, was unconvincing to them. I explained the system, that there must be a list, and they must follow instructions or they'd find trouble. I wasn't asked what trouble, but was treated to the usual ouzo.

Shortly after, from two of the villages, the *Proedros* (village head-man) rode down on his mule to my office with instructions in the official *katharevousa* (purified language) for me to explain, which I could do from my English copy. This became their habit with Government communications.

INTERPRETATIONS

I had an interpreter: his English was poor (Chicago eatery, I thought), his Greek sounded dubious, and I could see he hated the travelling. My Greek was coming on, and they liked to hear me, so I got him put on other work till they found a better. I had my clobber dyed chestnut-brown: khaki paid no dividends here. It became lighter and blotchy: the laundresses in the smaller places bashed it on stones in a stream, dried it in full sun, and it smelt fresher than soap powder claims.

KATAKHOI. A night in the malarial marshes, seemingly missed by the ubiquitous DDT sprays. Here, and at Aitoliki, like a fortress on its bridge over a shallow sea-lake, the KED (Central Distribution Committee) was working, but one village hostile. Told me we supported communists. A stupid remark, I said: we try to help the cold and hungry: you complain to the Nomarch if I put anyone on the list for politics, and I'll complain when you do the same - and be careful, for you know you do.

AGRINION.   A new interpreter presents himself, shifty-looking, a Kapetanios, he said: of a very small caique, I thought. On the first village meeting at a taverna under trees, the regular scene on these occasions: women headscarfed, spinning their yarn on hand bobbins in the shadows, I tried him out.   The complaint was about timber for rebuilding.   Tell them I agree that it was promised, and I'm sorry we've received none for any centre, and we voluntary workers can only ask again, which I will.   I listened: he referred to causing trouble, and the gentleman didn't have the stuff. "That is not what I said."   I spoke slowly in Greek, turned to them and explained it: the atmosphere completely changed.   I felt sorry for him; he said he was rather tired that morning.

KALAMOS.   Found the caique Minimay, sailing before dawn - which came up quickly in mist over the heights, then lit the sails and sea.   The crew made ersatz coffee laced with paraffin. I asked about the awful killing up the coast: Honour must be defended, one said, and the other seemed to agree.   Called at Kastos to drop a small load - a tiny island that seemed content and not worth wasting a day on, I thought.   A heron on a rock: you like to shoot it? I reject the offered gun, being for peace with nature as with man.   They laughed appreciative - of the quip, perhaps.   We towed a fishing boat in to Kalamos, dolphins sporting with us up the channel, then walked the springy planks, rock to rock and shore, balancing with pack and bedroll in either hand. Was offered hospitality by our captain Karfakis in his pleasant white house amongst similar in the village up the slope.   Neither would he accept payment for my passage.   The schoolmaster, French speaking, helped me, meeting the KED.   Everything OK, they said, no lists were needed.   No lists, I said, then no supplies: no school meals, no powdered milk.   They needed the rations and would see to it

MYTIKAS.   A fisherman took me, sailing like a silver swan, to the nose of sand, before the low white houses, vineyards. orange and olive groves with mountains behind: I wade ashore. Where is the place? (the usual phrase) I asked a local. Tilting his head in the negative sign, with a sweep of hand he followed the curve of silver sand. Yes, highest tide line, a low bank, was lined with sunbaked turds.

CIRCUMVENTING THE MANIPULATORS

The elders gathered in front of the taverna; one Maroulis, who had spent many years on Marseilles waterfront spoke French and offered to be my guide and interpreter as I needed - and space in his little house to sleep. We called a town meeting at 3 pm, after the siesta. I didn't trust this coterie and wanted things in the open. The house was minimal, but better than most of the simple two-roomers amongst the greenery that looked romantic from a distance. I ate a K-ration and he accepted one, and we took our siesta.

The Judge - self-styled, I suppose, introduced me, rather incorrectly, it seemed. I told M. not to bother with that, and explained my mission. He then assured me that the KED was working and all distributions up to date. I saw murmurs. I'd need to see the lists and hear any complaints. Altercations! The judge now said we were only waiting for the UNRRA man to come. We broke up in disorder. I made a note of loads of requests, fertiliser for vines, advice on irrigation included, and I could have extended them, seeing their rudimentary mattocks, ploughs, etc. The success was in breaking up that clique - also giving Maroulis, who seems honest and sensitive, some status. We shall meet again when they've settled down.

PIPEDREAMS

ARCHONDOCHORION, with lovely glimpses over the seven isles on the way between the mountains. First sight of it was like some eastern, high prairie settlement - an epitome of this region they call *Xeromeros*, dry or barren place. No teacher, doctor nor vehicle access; water cloudy from the cisterns of roof run-offs; about 1000 inhabitants. Men sit with worry-beads, some bubble-pipes; women outside the houses, shawled, twirling hand spinerettes. The headman going on about *I megali idea* (The great idea). A totally mad idea, I said, no one will support you, and anyway, historically Constantinople ruled Athens and not vice-versa. The shabby-looking priest said we needed a new St. Paul to lead us. A sceptic murmured to me that what they got was Zervas and his damned Andartes (right wing guerillas)! Most sat sourly with their ouzo. Families go to Mytikas for rations: those in poverty only? Of course! Yet some said no when I asked, others yes, and at present I cannot check. Back to Mytikas, I paid Maroulis. I'd have kept him on but he had his plot to cultivate. He was more footweary than I, and had become more politically enlightened by the trip, I think.

DANGERS, VERMINOUS AND POLITICAL

LEFKAS, by fast motor-caique, on its spit of marshy land and sea-channel with sunken Italian ship. Slightly Venetian, scruffy, with wooden upper stories propped across the narrow streets against the earthquakes; surface drains that stank. On the hotel wall some British squaddy, I presume, had painted 'Danger - bugs and rats': yes! Had *iachni*, a greasy stew, in the taverna with local non-resinated wine . A guy saw me buy *Eleftheria*, the KKE newspaper, and told me how communists are persecuted here. Of course. Talked with the Nomarch, in French, in the morning: new and inexperienced. Sounds like a muddle. I must return and spend more time. Sent a wire for Solon, the jeep and summer clothing, then took advantage of a caique to spend the weekend with Don Pitcher of the FAU in Ipiros.

PREVESA. Tea and talk in his digs, in which he has a collection of ikons, and he drove me the long, rocky road to Ionnanina, picturesque bulwark of a city jutting into the lake, dominated by the Pindus peaks. So met the rest, whose service was now ending. The area was fraught by tension: we heard shots in the night. A joy to have so much English talk, and share our animadversions on the future.

NEW FRIENDLY CONTACTS

AMPHILOCHIA. The hotel was grotty, offered no sheets, so after a letter-writing session with my lamp, just laid on the bed and slept. At morning coffee I was recommended a family up the hill so gladly went.

A mother and two daughters greeted me. I took to them as a second base. We were all up at 6 each day, mum straight off to work, the girls to get my coffee and that of Eftalie (another lodger who deals with our supplies at the Agricultural Bank, from whom I found my recommendation came) then watch me shave in the porch with the dribble of water from a ceramic urn with tap, hanging flat on the wall like a spirit-dispenser in a pub. They were off to the tobacco land, planting and watering all day. Yet they smile in the evening, walking barefoot up the zig-zag cobbled way from the town well with big water pitchers balanced on heads. The mum does my washing, river-stones and sun method. Two boys, when at home seem to laze about outside: husband is away, unspecified, maybe in the mountains. *Ach ..men!* she says disdainfully: she had an air of suffering and nobility - also a certain fatalism, so common here with those at the receiving end. After talking of events there will be a pause, then *ti na kanome?*, what can we do? - and *etsi enai i zoi*, thus is life. The house is bare, sunny and clean.

I start by visiting places along the coast. To a couple of villages I had to walk from the mountain track: desperately poor, no schools nor knowledge of a source of aid. Maybe healthier than the coast, though some old Anatolian refugee families still lived in cabins.

VONITZA. A French-spoken lawyer gave me house space and offered help. A good taverna in the tree-shaded square where we could eat and talk. After morning coffee he took me round the three-ring fort high up with lovely views across to Ipiros. The lovely little Byzantine church - but also the school: 250 kids crushed into 2 rooms; scabies, malaria, TB and glandular fever most prevalent. A meeting in the square after the siesta. At least we'll get children's milk started soon, and the marshes treated I hope. Before evening folk parade gently to and fro on the square, some families neatly dressed, not the really poor, of course, stopping to talk - and with me when I joined.

ALL COMMUNISTS HERE ?

Visited a few more mountain villages from here. Poverty, but few bother even to ask for relief. At one the priest said we're all communists here. Surely you can't be a KKE? I asked. All, all, he replied and laughed. They often ring the little church bell when I call, and the men come from the lands, including the priest in tatty biretta and kaftan, as poor as they are.

TALENTED AND DESTITUTE

AGRINION again, and a session on reports and letters. Also there were Nel, Dinah Green of the YWCA and Mary Hayward (UNRRA Health) in town, so was able to pass on some of my recommendations directly. Then Gretel arrived. I went with her and Nel to visit a sculptor, Christos, Nel had made contact with. Terrorised by the Andartes, he had fled and built himself a cabin in the marshes near Panaitolikon. She led us to it, a hovel really, where he subsisted, ragged, malarial and tubercular, on what food his mother could scrounge. He could rely on locals who knew him to keep their mouths shut, but they just scraped a living themselves under that regime, and two German soldiers who discovered him seemed friendly, so he wasn't disturbed. All round the patch among the reeds and rushes were sculptings and plaster casts, which looked good to me. He spoke good French, having studied in Paris till interrupted by the war, but no English, so Nel had been out of any discussion. We gave our spare rations and promised to try to get him to Athens with somewhere to exhibit.

DESPERATE, BUT WHAT MEASURES?

Next to MISSOLONGION again with no success. The Nomarch, after the elections, had simply fled, and the clerk admitted that, though he did his best, he could not control things.

Then ASTAKOS, with much the same result, and one despairs. I bathed and ate well, however, and it is a lovely drive despite the lack of any road surface. Limestone dales like Derbyshire: and when we had a break we disturbed an eagle with the remains of his chicken; he circled and returned. Solon pointed out the swallows - on their way to England. He nearly swamped us at the wobbly pontoon that replaces the bombed bridge across the Acheloös. It depends on a rope one hangs on to get the jeep aboard: coming off he accelerated too quickly and when the front wheels hit the bank I was left with just a toe-hold short of foundering the jeep and us.

FAIR ... BUT ...

The ELECTIONS were adjudicated fair by AMFOGE, the allied military force for observing Greek elections: i.e. a USA, British and French presence in each constituency. The taverna talk is that the Yankee spends his time seeking food and sociability, the Brit. getting fairly boozed and the Frenchie chasing girls, and as they had fascist interpreters, not much store was set by their observations.

NOT A LONE VOICE

There are two tavernas in Agrinion: the Rightist one has better food, but I make sure to visit the Leftist often enough to indicate my stance. There is some dissatisfaction with ELAS now, accusations that they fought more Greeks than Germans. I was emphasising that what bothers me is the indifference of both sides to the destitution of any but their own. Svolos, the government engineer, in town on a project for bringing electricity to Amphilochia. who was about to leave, sat down again and came in angrily supporting my case. He thought I should go again to Amphilochia, suggested I accompany him. He calls in the office if he sees me there.

MOUNTAIN VILLAGES

I decided to do a few more visits. without much hope of organising anything at present, and relying on Solon to tell me if roads were mined. This is where Solon's political affiliation and our mutual trust came in so usefully: he could find out where mines were in fact being laid so I made visits that others would have regarded as reckless. Solon had a kip in the jeep when I had to walk. He said I'm seen as a sort of Byron - not the most helpful image, if that is so.

BYRONIC GO-BETWEEN

One where he previously said he'd find out whether it was safe, I was keen to try again. Not in hope of doing anything for UNRRA, but I'd read of hostilities there and had a conceit that I might make a bid for direct peacemaking. He said he thought the road would be safe now. We had rugged 2-hour drive: tracks twisting between bare, rocky ridges and green ravines, with sudden glimpses of the sea and Seven Isles. Parked at a small khani (Turkish taverna) under the trees and got some rachi (similar to ouzo). Soon five men came down, we greeted, touching hands: the keeper brought more drink and introduced the spokesman. I checked that they knew who I am, then asked directly what's been happening.

They crept down in the night, he said, shot the headman and his family, and two men who were shouting, before we could do anything. I expressed my sorrow and horror - but of course you do the same sort of thing. Never in Holy Week, he said. Is murder so much different in this week? Murder? sir, this is war. A silence. He turned his beads. I mentioned the lovely landscape, and he asked about England. Then - would it be possible for me to go and speak with your enemies? The five talked briefly: not from here, we think you would be shot first sight. Firm handshakes then, and hearty *kalo Lambri*, good Easter.

GERMAN = FASCIST = NO GOOD

20 Apr. 46, to AMFISSA for lunch. Our Beatrice had already left for Patras. Were told in the taverna how they had blown up the public latrines because they were built by the Germans, so

had none now, and how the British Major draped in a red cloth and his detachment - only half drunk - with red flags paraded round the town on the news of the Labour election victory. At LIDHORIKION, a ghastly ruin left by the Germans, I was pestered by a family of Vlachs, fortune tellers, etc. I declined that but gave a small gift in exchange for tales of their winter hardships, sleeping rough.

A TRIP WITH CHRISTOS

At DELPHI we treated Christos to the only hotel, sharing my room, with views across the dark olive groves to the little port of Itea below and Galaxidhi on the opposite coast. He was surprised to find that Gretel and I were not salaried. We bought coloured eggs, feta, bread and wine for a gossip-meal with the women in their room.

The museum treasures were still safely buried. It was great to see with what rapture Christos fingered the bas-reliefs. *Ça vous rendra fou!* (would drive you mad) to try to achieve those lines. We had the whole site to ourselves, threading our way past the treasuries, the base of the great temple, theatre and outside to the remaining half of the stadium. With water from the spring of the Oracle at Castelli we had our packed lunch, bright red poppies on all banks and open spaces. A group from Athens in a clapped-out lorry joined us, shared their wine, then had us dancing on the road, which was surfaced here. Having been shown how a couple of times in Athens I was the star: of our foursome only.

STATISTICS, INTERPRETATION OF

PATRAS, May 1946. Charles had called a welfare conference. It was found that over 30% of the Greek population are drawing free rations. I suggested that in our areas more than that are destitute, but not nearly so many in fact receiving them, even if allocated. The problem is political, virtually still that of civil war. Our work is on the right lines, but the lines so thin that I wonder are they used as eyewash on the international scene.

A picnic lunch: talked to Lily Tempeli, Bea's interpreter, once a wretched, abused child of Lidhhoriki under the Germans, now educated and elegant. All to tea on the lawn with the colonel's family. Civilisation, eh?

THE VISITATION

AGRINION. Charles and Basil (his interpreter) arrived as arranged: met the inspector and agreed to visit the school tomorrow. The descent on it of five of us with staff car and jeep was impressive. So was Charles's talk, through Basil, to the poor, barefoot pupils on Abe Lincoln. Perhaps, wide-eyed, they thought this was the word of God they'd heard about.

PROPHYLACTIC PARANOIA

The account I gave him of Amphilochia made him wish to go straight to Lefkas, so we set off with a brief stop there for a snack. He had to share my room at the hotel and I was astonished that he puffed his bed with clouds of DDT which I resented breathing, and put chlorine tablets in the water carafe, astonished that I did not. We saw the Nomarchis, new and insecure. I kept quiet, let C. expound the scheme at some length, pleased with an assurance that it would be supported. He went on to suggest that perhaps we could get the colonel to visit and welcome him here. I asked Basil to mention the desperate poverty in the villages, and the April allocations were not yet received. (I'd spoken to the clerk). My implication was that perhaps the Colonel would be better engaged in straightening the kinks in the pipeline.

Their third visit was to be Missolongion. I asked to be excused, to spend more time here. Basil is competent, can take all this in his stride.

THE BISHOP CONDESCENDS

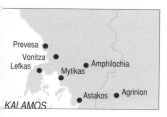

LEFKAS, June 46. An invitation from the Bishop (in French): pleasant, with smooth talk about the island and people - poor, yes, but contented and pleased to have our help. He could tell me more about the hospital's needs, so I went. ... We called a meeting of the KED in the Nomarchy, Bishop in the chair. Everyone agreed to carry out the full procedure, of course.

Kotsiris, the KED clerk, wanted to visit villages to familiarise himself and could speak good enough English to translate, so I was glad of him, for the dialect could baffle me. He had found a suitable girl as clerk in his office but the Bishop had objected; she was a communist. I interviewed her and wrote a formal note to the Nomarch - that I'd heard the KED had raised some objection on political grounds, a discrimination that UNRRA aid does not permit. Valid or not, it worked.

Saw Kotsiris for coffee: he had a lot to talk about. What infuriated him most was that he'd been told Theodora must go: they didn't have communists: there were hints about Solon also, and other problems with the KED. I interviewed her, said she must continue at work unless there's written notice. Then directly to the Nomarch. She's a communist, isn't she? I don't know and wouldn't ask: people's political opinions are their own business - I think my driver is, though he's an excellent driver, which is all that matters, so long as he stays within the law. We can't allow political discrimination in a democracy, you'll agree? His reply was not coherent, but she did not get notice. After we have left, you bet!

WHAT WAY AHEAD?

My letters home now were mainly on our family and future — one incidentally making clear that I do not *support* the communists: many of their acts are quite insupportable, and I don't fancy what would be imposed by them, any more than the trend of the present regime. Yet my sympathies are with those they claim, with justification, to represent, as they were with the fellahin in Egypt. It's a political dimension to our work, to which I see no political solution.

Back in PATRAS the colonel came and sat in my office (the first time, they said), angry to hear that the Government was asking Vol-soc personnel to leave - and here was I writing useful reports! He felt it was an insult and would like to put in a strong protest from us. He had no illusions about the way the government was going, and no enthusiasm for the return of the King — agreed with my contention that he'd win the plebiscite, as too many people would be afraid to vote against. I said I'd call a meeting of all our field workers. We were united for carrying on: Beatrice and Gretel (IVSP), Dinah and Monica (YWCA), Margaret (SCF), and the UNRRA folk.

"HOW FAR THAT LITTLE CANDLE ..."

Monica Walters asked me to visit KALAVRITA again. I slept under an apple tree, the ripe ones thudding around me in the night, after a meal in the plateia [square] by acetylene lamps - symbol of great improvements. It was good to see a few men working, coopering for the vintage, etcetera, and women still dressed like crows, husking maize. I met the committee and congratulated them: will try to get more timber, lamps, storage vessels.

SCOUTS' HONOUR

On their patron saint's day the Boy Scouts asked me to a feast at their camp with all the dignitaries. I got a very British howl of welcome from each patrol, and walked with some to a mountain monastery. Stopped at a taverna on the return; driver Perikleos complimented me on my speech: I had prepared it, emphasising the international aspect of both our organisations, and the folly of further war. Did you notice the black looks of the Nomarch and one or two more? he asked.

THANK YOU AND GOODBYE

ATHENS had called a conference of Vol-socs' members. There were chasing, shouting demos from each side in town, the police in battle order. The purpose of the government in calling us amounted to an apology for the peremptory way our dismissal came out, and an assurance our services were valued - until October, at least, when they hoped to have their own system working.

For IVSP I'd fixed an appointment with minister Doxiades, the only one with vision, I'd heard said, and member of the UNO council for reconstruction. Jumping off the non-stop, mantrap chain of lifts, I enquired for his office. Where did you learn that communist language? my respondent asked, evidently a high-up. It's what all the Greeks whom I meet speak, I said, and he coldly directed me.

The minister was positive, confirming the value of groups like ours in stimulating the acceptance of the needed reconstruction here, was interested in our submissions, made notes of our talk and clipped them into the folder he already had. He knew of our (and my) reports. I thought I'd have more explaining to do but he was fully briefed. On leaving I mentioned that Athens seemed excited about the plebiscite. He said he felt like the only one who wasn't!

Returned to PATRAS to find the Nomarch is appointing committees by police districts for welfare supplies, claiming the KEDs are failing. What price honesty and democracy now? Some seventy displaced persons repatriated from Italy: our folk did well to find them lodgings; now the police are moving them on. What odds that these are the secret royalist battalion to support the royalists? There are further reports of fighting in the Pindus.

ECCLESIASTICAL AUTHORITY

ZAKINTHOS, or Zante. The Bishop (or maybe archbishop), great voice of authority here, wanted to see me tomorrow. There were many royalist posters, *erchetai* (he will come), which is now a fact.

The talk with his reverence was a questionnaire, in good English. What did I think of the Slav question? It's not Slav but political and military power that exploits nationalism. Would it not be better to get on and finish the war? Surely we have had enough of that calamity: consider Hiroshima, the size of Athens - it could be repeated a hundred times, and who could benefit? Surely UNRRA should not give them food? Give whom? The communists. I'm not of your faith, but what about the call to feed the hungry? And when folk who are starving turn to communism they have my sympathy rather than those who refuse to help. I explain my badge: we seek to help all oppressed in the hope for peace.

He lost interest, this august, bearded and kaftanned figure with the strong bass voice of authority here, and although president of the welfare centre, who signed their requisitions, he had only superficial knowledge of their working.

CLEARING UP

Oct. 46   My reports are brief and pointed. I sign what Petras asks me to, checking that it is within my province. There are signs of winter: my stored clothes had been burgled, so I had to ask the police. They found them at once at the parents' of a lad who'd been employed to sweep, etc., and returned them apparently untouched. They found him too, and said he wouldn't do that again. Felt sorry for him: he couldn't read the label with my name. The Colonel looked in, pleased I was not rushing off: told him of the state of things and of my evidence of the Royalist terror, and of Christos the sculptor whom we planned to get to Athens, which he approved. So I got the 15cwt truck with Solon as driver.

15th, the end of our remit. The Colonel had made an appointment with the Nomarch to protest; it could only be formal for he was no friend: he hardly commented, but talked about future plans. The Colonel mentioned my discussion with the minister, but we agreed not my plan concerning Christos.

Nov. 46. Typed my last official communications to UNRRA, the ministry and IVSP. A farewell evening in the mess for the end of welfare in Region C: I the last Vol-soc worker to depart.

Doxiadis called me to the ministry: good of him with all the problems he has to face, encouraging us with submission of future proposals. He asked me to let him have a memo of this discussion, so went to UNRRA and typed one with a copy for Derek in London. Kept calling in at Transport. That ship is full, so not calling at Piraeus: there's another about the 12th. You'll get me there by Christmas? Should do, no guarantee, don't keep bothering us. So took a few days leave.

THE ONE-CARD TRICK

Put up at the scruffy Lord Byron Hotel at ARGOS. Learnt of trucks going south in the morning. Two were full, overfull. The third was the mail, and riding with it was forbidden — except for Dr. 2000 it seemed, and promise not to smoke ... Hailed a Daimler, or what had been, OK to SPARTA, eight bodies within, packages piled on a roof-rack and my pack looped over the headlamp. Put up at the nasty hotel. Had to be nice to a half-drunk soldier threatening with a tommygun his mate, whom I told to shut up, whatever it was about. I walked out to MISTRA. At the hotel the tommygun character asked me for my ID card. Showed him my UNRRA one. No good, he said, English. It's good for the Nomarch and Government, you'd better be careful. What are you, archaeologist? Yes, I pointed to the word 'organisation' - see, *archiologikos*. Later two soldiers arguing, raising rifles. I did the card trick, flashed it and said sternly, that's illegal, put the guns down, indicating the wall behind. One did, the other cleared off, cursing. The potheads of the army.

The 12th approaching, yet they deflected inquiries about the ship. No use being furious with UNRRA here, it seems, and would cost more to cable and wait. I went round Piraeus waterside offices for anything to Italy or Marseilles: maybe. Next thought of Greek airways. Spun my story: what about...he called his mate.

Yes, could have free lift on special plane to fetch some big pot from Rome. Good, when? It leaves in two hours, he said, you need an exit permit. They were moving the gangway as I staggered across the concrete. They shoved it back. Flying over all the spots I knew in Region C, shining in the sun. Fog over the Appenines: where are we, I heard the co-pilot say. We'll go down, and they did, close to the smoky peaks, then up again.

ROME. UNRRA couldn't provide transport, but I could stay at the hotel: surely Athens could have done better, she said. Next morning I went to the station, the British RTO. Yes, a leave train to Florence : but cancelled. Tried the USA one. Yes, a leave train overnight to Como: booked without question. Ordered off train at frontier for documents to be checked; two of us stamped up and down to keep warm in front of the office till they called us in - and then had time to phone Gretel at Berne - a delightful visit; also to Willi and Dora in Zurich, and got a ticket to PARIS. Took the metro to Place de la République, to UNRRA without much hope. But they were quite appalled at my treatment. Booked me in dinner, bed and breakfast at L'hôtel de la République, and a movement order, first class to London. Got most of my francs changed for a ten-bob note. Then Calais, Dover: the ticket inspector said you shouldn't be coming this way. It's the way I was sent: but I knew what he meant: you haven't got that first class look about you, scruffy greatcoat, boots! But here we were. first class to dear old Victoria, evening, in a pea soup fog just as we had left, and me having got, in carefree English, someone to change the ten-bob note, standing shivering in the queue outside a telephone box.

What had we achieved? how successful was it all? Impossible to say, though it had its rewards in at least temporarily aiding some people. Perhaps more important, I know I gained a practical contempt for wealth and power as an aim in life, and respect for the practical possibilities of co-operation and peace amongst the poor and oppressed. And that, I think, is a significant part of the purpose of our groups.

ITALY

*Phyllis Rate
(Unit 3)*

A SHORT, INTENSE EXPERIENCE

We attended courses in Egypt, and took over vehicles and equipment issued to a Relief and Rehabilitation Unit, becoming RRU 5. Some of the training was useful and some not - we never did have to pitch our little tents! Not being a linguist, I came to regret that we had so little time to learn Italian after spending so much on Serbo-Croat. My most abiding memory of Egypt is the appalling poverty we saw outside our privileged camp at Maadi, which left me with a lasting concern for its relief.

When RRU 5 arrived in Bari early in 1945, the war in southern Italy had been over for more than 6 months. First the Allied Military Government, then the Allied Commission, and now the United Nations (UNRRA) were organising relief for the civilian population. Our uniforms and status made us privileged, and although the people we worked *with* knew that we were civilians, I doubt if those we worked *for* realised that we were any different from the thousands of others of many nationalities who had passed their way before.

The clothes that came to our warehouse were tightly packed in huge bales; they were crumpled and often quite unsuitable. After some months I came to the conclusion that America should have sent some sewing machines, bales of cloth and plenty of needles and cotton.

Another member of the team told me years later that he knew that the consignment of unsuitable men's shoes he had distributed had found their way on to the black market, but had decided that it was the best place for them - at least the refugees got a little cash.

The Abruzzi had been a very poor area before the war, and this may indeed have helped the resourceful peasant families who returned to re-build their lives. I still have the greatest admiration for their fortitude and endurance in their daunting work.

In the late autumn a project was organised which was more like a traditional SCI service. A group of students from Rome University joined us to remove rubble from the centre of Francavilla, a few miles up the coast, and lay it as hard-core for a road to an isolated village. From this developed the Italian branch of SCI. *[p 70]*

SNAPSHOT - TARANTO: PROBLEMS

Cara Rablen (Unit 3)

In January 1945 our job was to register the Italian refugees displaced by the war as it moved steadily north. We quickly learned to be on our guard. Italian peasant women do not take their husband's surname, so both husband and wife would attempt to register the family! One of the objects of registering the families was to distribute clothing in due course. A lot of the adult clothing sent from America was totally unsuitable. Italian peasant women tend to be short and rather solid and only wear black once they are married. The clothing was for tall, slim women and was brightly coloured. However, children's garments were more acceptable, also clothing for men. Mostly they did not normally wear shoes, but were glad to have them to be buried in.

A PERSONAL RECOLLECTION

Denys Kay-Robinson (Unit 3)

The first thing to be remarked about the IVSP Italy team is that it should never have been there at all. Until the last moment of our training period in Egypt we were destined for Yugoslavia, and it was only when Tito had finally triumphed over his rival Mihailovic and gave out that he was interested purely in medical teams that we were switched to southern Italy - the *Mezzogiorno* as the Italians call it. So after battling to master even the rudiments of the formidable Serbo-Croat language, we had to set to work to see just how much Italian we could assimilate in what seemed to us no time at all. We also speculated on how much of the training in self-sufficiency and 'living rough' that we had undergone would prove of use in this very different country. (In fact, quite a lot of it did.)

The weather in the Mediterranean was sunny and warm, enabling us to spend long periods on deck studying our Italian and drying our washing, but to our dismay Taranto greeted us with icy conditions and snow on the ground. After as cold a night as I can ever remember, we drove our trucks to our first destination, a small coastal resort near Bari. Each morning we had to drive into Bari for our work, which consisted initially of helping the very new Italian government to sort out the swarms of refugees who had fled the war in other parts of Italy, and in particular from its now lost colonies.

Bari.

The thrill of repatriation was brought home to me one morning when I looked out of an upper window and saw a large open truck parked on the other side of the street and piled high with all kinds of domestic possessions, on to and in among which the happily chattering family were finding niches to instal themselves for the drive home.

We also distributed second-hand clothes from America to those in need, until it became evident that to continue this task adequately, it would be much more practical to instal distribution centres in various towns farther south. Accordingly the diaspora of the Italy unit took place: we (and this applied also to the other voluntary organisations that had been working alongside us in Bari) were split up into pairs, each pair with at least one vehicle, and sent to various chief towns of departments. We heard that two members of the Save the Children Fund, both fervent Welsh nationalists, bewildered the good people of the town they were sent to by displaying a large Red Dragon banner outside their billet. I myself was sent with Hugh Horsfield to Taranto, hot and very different from when we had first encountered it. Here, apart from working hard at our mission, we were lucky in being able to make some good Italian friends among our helpers and the rural officials. This pleased us for more than just personal considerations.

Our job in Taranto was by no means sedentary: we had occasion to drive out to a number of villages, and once I drove our 3-ton truck to Naples and back to fetch supplies - scores of miles along mostly unrepaired secondary mountain roads with daunting gradients and hairpin bends so sharp that the truck had to be reversed halfway round in order to complete the turn. Furthermore every other town and village along the way was having a religious procession. Progress was not rapid.

Among the pleasures I recall in Taranto was lying in bed on many hot nights and hearing, through our open window and theirs, someone exquisitely playing Chopin and Schubert on the piano. But in due course it was back to Bari, and thence to Ortona-a-Mare, in which, and all its satellite villages, there were more damaged - and frequently destroyed - buildings than undamaged. Reconstruction was proceeding at a snail's pace owing to shortage of money and an almost complete absence of transport. (It was quite normal to see such few commercial vehicles as existed trundling along with no tyres.)

Our office and billet were in a large mansion in the town centre that had been half demolished by shelling. A further part of it even collapsed on one of us, fortunately without causing serious injury, but the rest was sound and roomy enough, and also the plumbing was working! The men's bedroom, which we soon turned into 'Home' with our camp beds, led on to a landing that gave access to a loo and stone staircase that in turn led down in to a small cellar. This was the nocturnal sportsground for what appeared to be all the rats in Ortona. Mercifully - and puzzlingly - none of them came upstairs, but the noise they created made it quite difficult to get to sleep until one grew used to them, and a night visit to the loo was always an adventure.

THE FIRST TRAIN HOME

Hugh Horsfield (Unit 3)

(Extracted from a report, an abridged form of which appeared in the Manchester Guardian Weekly, 10th August 1945)

This is the story of the first train returning refugees from the Province of Taranto in the south to their home towns in the former battle zones of central Italy. The word 'train' is perhaps a little misleading for an assembly of 14 covered goods wagons which was hitched to a variety of goods trains to make a halting progress northwards, but a train is what we always called it.

The return to their homes of some 30,000 Italian refugees, scattered over nine provinces of Southern Italy, is being organised by about 30 young British volunteers, members of the Friends' Ambulance Unit, the Save the Children Fund, Catholic Relief and IVSP. Dispersed over Taranto province, there are some 2,500 refugees and at the moment six voluntary relief workers. Of these five are engaged practically full time on a distribution to refugees of clothes supplied by UNRRA and Italian and American relief organisations. The train was originally planned for May 25th [1945] and was to return 400 priority workers, peasants and

artisans, with their families, to two camps at Ortona and Termoli for dispersal in the provinces of Aquila, Chieti and Campobasso. Owing to congestion in these dispersal camps, the date of the train was postponed to June 6th, and a few days later, advanced to June 3rd. In the meantime I had been looking for premises, in which 400 refugees could be accommodated, prior to loading on to the train. There was nothing suitable at first. Two olive oil factories, not working during the summer, were requisitioned, which with a good bit of adaptation and screening of machinery could shelter 140. Then a building, formerly a monastery, was derequisitioned by the military, at Martina Franca. This had been used under the Fascist regime as a holiday home for children and could provide excellent accommodation for 200 refugees. Then we might squeeze a hundred or so more into the big school at Castellaneta, which was already housing permanently 350 refugees. Michele, our young Italian clerk, was getting out a list of all the refugees in the priority occupations. Then we received a notice that the military had placed a ban on the return of refugees to Ortona and Pescara, so out went so many. A couple of days later a ban went on for Castel di Sangro and eight other communes where a large proportion of the houses had been destroyed. So out went several dozen more families from our list. Less than ten days to train time. Found Michele had included in the priority occupations only farm workers, tailors, cobblers and carpenters. Got him on the transfer *urgentissimo* of builders and stone masons from the non-priority list. Even then with so many towns being banned, we hadn't the train complement of 400 so we added those of the non-priority occupations who had houses standing to which they could return.

Monday May 29th

Produced my list of refugees to be collected at two centres from nine different communes.   First difficulty - how to get the news out.   No telephones, lists too long to send by telegraph, too urgent to be sent by ordinary post. No motor transport available to take a special messenger round.   The provincial medical officer had a car but no tyres. No one else had a car. In the end we found the police would provide two motor cyclists, so Bonifaccio missed his lunch, getting the lists typed out for each commune, and by four o'clock they were on their way.

Wednesday May 30th.

A telegram that Polish soldiers were now moving into the monastery which is to house 70 of our refugees. Off by lorry to Martina Franca, but get held up by the Taranto swing bridge, which is open to shipping three times a day. Lorry engine making a horrible grating noise when starting up, but after a quarter of an hour it runs normally. Hope it isn't going to pass out. Arrive half an hour late. Polish military requisition has priority over our Italian civilian requisition, but we get them to postpone their occupation until Monday, promising that all our refugees will move out on Sunday. Delivered some palliasses, soap, crockery and cutlery. Hurry back the twenty miles to Taranto, and get over the swing bridge eight minutes before it is due to open.

Thursday May 31st.

Departure day minus three. Lots of refugees wanting to go back home, but not on the lists because they were not priority workers or else had their homes in the banned communes. Conceded a few places to old grandmothers etc. who could not very well be left behind when their relations returned, but generally had to be heartless. One old farmer, grey stubble on his face, jumped on the running board as I drove off - he had two houses, an invalid son, someone else was blind. Nothing doing, his commune was on the banned list.

Friday June 1st.

D-day -2. The old stubble face with two houses and invalid son has turned up to repeat his tale. Still don't know who it is who is blind. "It pleases me not, but the commune is forbidden to all." Found Riette and Kathleen, two members of Catholic Relief, had arrived in a 15cwt truck. Their job is to travel up north with every refugee train from Southern Italy, dealing with any injuries, illnesses, new babies or other emergencies that may occur on the journey. On their first trip the engine got derailed; on another a box of biscuits from some American soldiers caused a struggle, in which half a dozen cut their hands on the sharp edges of the tin.   In the late afternoon to the office of the Director of Refugees and found that the hired lorry which should have taken food supplies to the monastery at Martina and then collected up refugees from 6 communes had failed to appear.   It should turn up tomorrow and also one loaned by the Italian Navy.

Saturday June 2nd.

One day to go.   Tearing off the May leaf from the calendar my wife sent me last Christmas, I saw for June "The gem cannot be polished without friction, nor man perfected without trials. - Chinese." This consoling wisdom from far away could not have been more timely.

The Poles afraid we should not be out in time for the reception there of some hundreds of Polish girls recently liberated in Germany.   Assured them we should have all the refugees out on Sunday afternoon.   Five minutes later, Donald arrives, having come out from Taranto in our 3-ton lorry.   A message has come through to Denys by phone from Bari: "As Ortona camp has received 800 unexpectedly from Northern Italy, you can send off only the 60 going to Termoli camp."   Snakes and ladders!   30 hours to train time, some 300 people with all their possessions being gathered up, and only 60 can go!   Well: assume for the time everything goes as originally planned, and so finish giving the details of the issue of food and travel passes and the collection by lorry tomorrow.   Everyone feeling a bit sick.   This done we all pack on to the lorries and hare off to the nearest phone.   On the way a private car dashes blindly out of a side street and hits us fairly amidships.   Much noise, its own bumper bent, but no damage to us.   Through narrow old streets with only three inches to spare on each side to the central telephone exchange as the line is clearest from there.   A sweet faced, long haired girl of about 15, in a high whitewashed room, sitting in front of a diminutive switchboard.   A wide-eyed boy of five watching her.   "Urgentissimo, Bari" says the Town Clerk.   It takes three quarters of an hour to get through.   At intervals our maiden suddenly flies into shrieking rage and screams a torrent of abuse at some other little girl sitting at a switchboard a dozen miles off.   And abruptly is calm, and we go on eating our sandwiches and drinking the vermouth brought in by an Italian woman, who has lived in Cairo, and who likes the English.   At last through to Peter at the Bari office. "No, no; the message was wrong, what Ortona camp had said was that they could take all our refugees except for about 100 for San Pietro, where there is trouble in billeting." Much relieved, can send off 200 or so instead of 60.

The Navy truck is bringing in only ten at a time because there is so much baggage, and will be all night on the job. Go to look at it and find it in a side street, the driver gloomily contemplating the bodywork. He says the last lot damaged it and he will get the blame. Dilapidated old bus anyhow; suggest putting a policeman in the back, and persuade him to go off for another lot. As we set off on our way back to Taranto, old stubble face hangs on the back for a hundred yards, panting about two houses, invalid son, someone else … I try to feel sorry for him, but he is a nuisance. About nine when we get back.

<u>Sunday June 3rd</u>.

Departure Day. A hotel boy brings a message to me in the bedroom as I dress. "Please do not repeat not entrain the 60 refugees destined for Termoli as Termoli Transit Camp already has 150 refugees above capacity". Don't enjoy breakfast. On the blower to Peter "What's the matter with Gilbert at Termoli?" "160 refugees from Milan arrived without warning, he can't possibly take any more." This time I agree the only possible thing to do is to hold my Taranto people back. Have a discussion with the Refugee Director on the distasteful job of separating the 60 who can't go from the 300 or so who can. Decide to keep all the people from Laterza back, about 80, as this will also help to relieve the numbers at Ortona. He writes to the Mayor of Castellaneta authorising him to accommodate the Laterza refugees in the school until they can be sent north on a later train. Go off to lunch and find the six lorries with their Indian drivers have arrived early and are blocking the road. Have difficulty in moving them on as the corporal in charge knows very little English and no Italian. Then Kathleen goes off with the Indians to collect the refugees at Martina Franca; we still don't know exactly how many have been assembled there. Riette, Donald and I in the 3-tonner go off to Castellaneta. Get to the school about four. There they are very pleased to tell me that they got everyone collected up last night, though it was one in the morning when the last ones arrived. (That Navy driver deserves a medal, though no doubt he will prefer 20 English cigarettes).

Back to the station, farewells in process, old women weeping, men kissing one another, an accordion being played. Only some *mothers sitting still and quiet, with sleeping babies in their arms. It begins to get dark. We get a message in battered English by telegraph from the worried Railway Transport Officer, who says he is sending up ten empty wagons on the train and will we get people on board as quickly as possible. He drives up shortly afterwards in a light truck to give any help he can. Very decent of him. He is very English, speaks shocking Italian without the slightest diffidence and will never learn more. A shindy outside and a porter and a refugee bustle in with a lot of relations. Turn out the relations; apparently the refugee was asleep near the track of an approaching train and, misunderstanding the porter who woke him up, started to fight him. Last minute appeals for permission to take all kinds of unlisted relatives. One old boy wants to discuss the price of my consent. Listen to all the appeals and turn them all down, knowing very well that quite a few will nevertheless travel.*

We have put on 154 here, so altogether we have 224 plus an unknown number of stowaways. The guard appears, someone had pinched his lamp. he can do nothing without it. The RTO goes back with him, I go forward and get on the footplate of the locomotive with the driver and fireman. A couple of blasts from the whistle and we are off. Stars bright above, the banking engine in the rear, glaring like a volcano. Keep stopping to take water, to shunt goods wagons or to let other trains pass. It begins to get light. Sitting on a locker, I go to sleep. When they wake me, we are at Bari. Our engine is uncoupled and another takes its place. Five minutes later, I watch the refugee train disappearing in the distance. Two hundred and twenty four souls going back to start life over again in the wreckage of their old homes. God help them.

Set off for the Bari office to see when we can forward the unfortunate 80 who were left behind.

SNAPSHOTS - LIVING - AND DYING

HH

CERRETO, MIGLIANICO, CHIETI, August 1945. Family of seven living for a year in one-room hut without window. Roof of loose boards with bits of tarred felt held down with bricks. New home under construction next door.

MORECINE, ORTONA, CHIETI, 28/8/45. House in front line for 6 months, just by a German battery. When 2 brothers and their families returned to the ruins, they found their fields were full of mines. The brothers had to remove these themselves. One got killed, but Giuseppe, the other, removed over 100 mines by attaching a long cord and pulling. We carried tiles to make a temporary roof for the two rooms occupied by the families.

CLEARING THE GROUND

From *Letter to Derek Edwards 8/11/93*

Lal Hardstone (Unit 3)

When the war in Europe was over the IVSP team moved to the Abruzzi. The FAU was before us and had already organised a transport team with American ex-army trucks (written off by US Army, but some viable, and the others could be used for spares) supplied by UNRRA to carry building materials. So IVSP came to Ortona (officially 80% destroyed if my memory is correct) found themselves a house, part of which later collapsed and nearly killed Henry Rablen, and settled in with some FAU men. The British army had taken over the former municipal sportsground as a vehicle depot and erected Nissen huts, and we inherited that. Italian drivers were recruited and their wages paid by UNRRA. I do not know how many thousands of tons were distributed around the area. No doubt all the records have been lost long ago.

The transport depot which FAU/IVSP had set up was still running in August 46 when I left Italy. By then, however, its importance had been recognised and an Italian Government Authority, headed by a civil engineer, set up to organise reconstruction of the war devastated areas. I remember being called to Rome and introduced by an UNRRA official to a high ranking Italian who was either in charge of or about to set up the Authority (*Comitato Autonome per il Secorso ai Senzatetti - CASAS - a convenient acronym since casa is the Italian word for house or home: senzatetti = homeless*) who wanted to know what we were doing and what facilities we had in Ortona.

It was towards the end of '45 that IVSP traditions were at last able to show themselves. A group of students from Rome was brought together at Ortona and some genuine pick and shovel work undertaken. The job was to remove the debris of the bombed buildings in the trucks to clear the sites for rebuilding. The rubble itself was taken out to the countryside where it was used to make roads. But this time we did not just supply the lorries, we supplied the labour, while local people looked on open mouthed to see people doing something which no one had got round to thinking of doing for themselves, and doing it for nothing! *[See Francavilla, below]*

There is one memory which must be included. In the rubble of some municipal building Jinny unearthed a sculptured *fasces* (the Fascist emblem) and called to Henry working nearby "Just look at the fasces I've got here". Henry mistook the word and said "Never mind - leave it, I'll clear it up".

FRANCAVILLA[*]

William B Thompson (Unit 3)

We'd been in Italy since the February of '45. We'd been based in Santo Spirito, in Ortona, and in various provincial capitals of the Mezzogiorno. We hadn't yet used either pick or shovel. We'd spent much time on administrative work, clothing distribution, and the organization of transport of materials to rebuild destroyed homes on the Cassino line. We longed to fulfil both the pick-and-shovel message of our beret badges and the 'I' of our initials.

IVSP is much more than just a relief agency, important as such agencies are. Were we in fact creating out of the devastation and turmoil of war something which would continue to provide for and inspire future generations of the people of the country we were working with and for?

'Cf Friedland, p 121

Italy (except in the North) had not gained that spiritual tempering from a Resistance movement, as had so many countries of Europe. All too many Italians still wanted the Allies to remain to save them from - they knew not what! Some might say 'Communism' (or even 'Tito'!) - perhaps the truth was to save them from themselves. That passivity had somehow to be done away with. The people had little or no confidence in their own local government machinery, and were all too ready to rely on the might·of the Allies - after a couple of decades relying on 'The might of Fascism'. For Italy had had a much longer period of regimentation to overcome than other countries, excepting perhaps those of the Soviet Union.

In order to try and overcome the passivity I've mentioned and at the same time to try and counteract the imbalance of administration in our work, I found myself after the summer of '45 addressing in the University of Rome a crowded meeting called by the Student Representative Council at my request. The novel idea to them of a pick-and-shovel scheme with student volunteers during their vacation was received enthusiastically. In November this idea became a reality.

We, the IVSP party, were ten in number; sixteen students came in two groups, each group for ten days, to our centre in Ortona. They lived with us in the bombed building we occupied as our headquarters. sharing billets, rations, and work.

At 8 o'clock each morning we set off by truck to Francavilla, a very badly damaged town some miles away near the Adriatic coast. There we worked with pick and shovel until 5 o'clock in the evening, with a short break for lunch.

The job we'd selected was clearing the rubble of a ruined church which had blocked the way into the Town Hall, then being rebuilt. In three weeks we shifted about 1000 tons of rubble, taking it into the neighbouring countryside to form a road where there had only been a mud track to some peasants' cottages.

In this work peasant volunteers joined with the students and us. A further source of help came from the children, who enthusiastically joined in the sorting of bricks as soon as they came home from school, or, what was more frequent, when playing truant. Altogether we built about a kilometre of road, as well as clearing a way through to the Town Hall. The good bricks which we salvaged were transported to Ortona, there to build a sand-pit for the kindergarten of a Convent School.

Working together, not just Italians and British volunteers, but men students and women students, and students with peasants, was something quite new and extraordinary in the experience of most of them, as indeed was the idea of students doing manual work at all! So, too, for the students, who had lived in Rome, was the contact with conditions of life in the distressed areas of a battle zone. And to find teachers joining in the same kind of work was unprecedented.

The full value of this particular service could only be realized some while after its close. For instance, through students who had been at Ortona others heard of this service, were impressed by what they heard, and wanted to take part in future services.. The result was the formation of an Italian branch of Service Civil International amongst the students of Rome - the first of two legacies for the future of Italy of the work of IVSP Unit 3. The second was the foundation of the Italian Youth Hostel Association (AIG), but that is another story.

SEPTEMBER 1946

Elsa Leman (Unit 3)

This Unit, which began life as UNRRA Italian Reconstruction Unit No 1, is now known as the UNRRA/CASAS Reconstruction Unit, Ortona. CASAS is the Italian Government organisation for rehousing. The voluntary societies involved in the Unit are: IVSP (British and Swiss); American Friends Service Committee; and Brethren Service Committee (also American).

We have been learning the ways of other nationals and hearing them discussing problems from a different point of view. With the Americans we have had interesting discussions on the race problem which is giving them much food for thought.

We assist with repair and rebuilding of houses, by providing free transport for materials, and by operating a scheme of 'anticipated materials': where the owner cannot afford them, purchase money is advanced by the commune in anticipation of the compensation which will be paid by the Government.

We (called 'negotiators' for the purpose and trusted as impartial) inspect the premises and if requests are reasonable arrange for transport. The whole family takes part in rebuilding. I have been amazed and horrified to see the way some people are living among the ruins of their homes - frequently in a ground floor room with the ruins of the top floors piled above; or in top back rooms reached by climbing over the debris of the front.

The villages are built on the tops of the hills, with the houses pressed closely together, so that the streets are narrow and there is no open space at the back. It is often quite difficult to pick out a village from the opposite side of the valley because of the grey stone of which the houses are built. It is the custom of the people to sit out in the street at all hours of the day, mostly with the chairs facing *inwards* as though they were extending the room into the street.

Bullock carts are used in the valleys, but higher up the mountain side donkeys carry the burdens. All over the place, however, women can be seen with loads of up to 100 lbs balanced on their heads. In the early morning a stream of women carrying round baskets in this way brings produce to Ortona market.

The general impression is not one of extreme want, and this year's good harvest has ensured the continuation of the basic ration throughout the winter. 80% of the people receive parcels from America - the little girls' big bows and frilly frocks are gifts from father, uncle or some other relative. But whatever the difficulties these people are able to burst into song on the slightest provocation and to enjoy their frequent festas with childlike zest.

VILLAGGIO DEL FANCIULLO

LANCIANO April 1947

EL

Boys' Town - 120 boys, from six to sixteen - one of a number of similar institutions teaching sharing and helpfulness to others, a lesson which these boys are learning rapidly and are happy to put into practice. For example: some of them brought a blind man into the Villaggio the other day and he was given shelter, food and some clean clothes. It was good to see how the boys went out of their way to talk to him and help him find his way about.

This transformation is the more remarkable when it is remembered that the Villaggio only began at the end of 1946, and that the first citizens were boys who, banded together under leaders of their own age, had been living by robbing Army trucks and pilfering from local farms.

On Christmas Eve 1946 Don Guido Visendez, an ex-Army chaplain, came to Lanciano at the request of the police to try to control this band of homeless ragged menaces to the countryside.

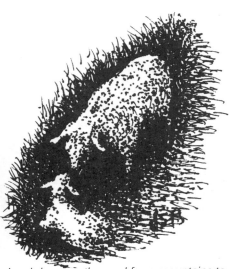

They were sons of servicemen killed or taken prisoner, and of men and women who had died during bombardments or been shot in reprisal raids. Their homes were heaps of rubble.

The boys had been collected by the police in the stables of an abandoned barracks, where Don Guido found them sleeping huddled together on the brick floor, some with arms round stray dogs they had adopted.

Don Guido and the boys, working side by side, have built the present Villaggio. Materials were brought by the boys from neighbouring ruined buildings and a two-storied building was created containing all the elements of a village.

The day begins at 6.45: breakfast is at 7.30: classes begin at 8.00. Each boy spends half the

Lamb born on the road from mountains to plains near Chieti

day in school and half in the workshop of his choice: carpenter's, blacksmith's or shoemaker's. There are three teachers taking classes I to V, elementary grade. Many of the bigger boys can scarcely read or write and are not sent to school in Lanciano.

My job is to keep clothes on the boys' backs. We have not enough clothing to give each boy his own wardrobe, and we are obliged to change the clothes of one group, wash and mend them and put them back on the next group. Shoes and socks are almost non-existent.

The affairs of the Villaggio are governed by a Mayor and Council elected by the boys. One evening recently I witnessed decision-making at the Assemblea Popolare. The matter under discussion was the re-instatement of a boy who had run away. His mother had begged Don Guido to take him back; this Don Guido refused to do unless the boys wished to have him back. The Mayor, Giuseppe Di Loreto, fifteen years of age, put it to the vote. "But," he said, "don't say 'yes' because everybody near you does; you must know why you are saying 'yes'". He asked some of the boys why they had voted in favour; one of the reasons given was that he had worked hard all the winter to prepare the house and therefore it was his home too.

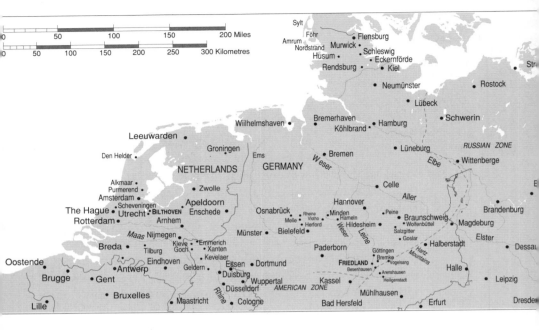

RELIEF ABROAD - II

When the request came for relief teams to be prepared for service in N.W.Europe it was found that the monies that IVSP had set aside for relief work were now so depleted that the Executive Committee, hard as it was to do so, came to the conclusion that it would have to tell COBSRA that whilst it had the personnel it simply did not have the money to finance further teams.

The teams in the Middle East had been, in the meantime, gaining a very good reputation for the work they were doing, and the reaction from COBSRA and some of the other organisations to the news that we could not see our way to sending a team in the "first European wave" was encouraging: they pressed IVSP to see if, in any way, the decision could be reconsidered; and also around this time there was news that the Treasury was likely to be going to give organisations £1 for every pound they spent. The result of this was that the committee met again and it was suggested that each member would write on a slip of paper how much they could "underwrite" if an emergency arose before the Treasury grant came through. The result of that exercise was that another letter was sent to COBSRA accepting the invitation to send a team and preparations were put in hand to assemble and prepare "UNIT 4".

DE

NETHERLANDS

Letter, 6/5/45, Finlay J McLaren (Unit 4) to his brother Alastair.

TILBURG 4TH MAY 1945

Liberation! To fully appreciate the meaning and depth of this word I think you must have suffered under an army of occupation. We have done the next best thing and lived in a recently liberated area where almost everyone had relatives still in occupied territory and so to some extent were able to share in the sheer joy that the radio announcement brought on Friday evening.

We were just beginning to rehearse a few songs for a sing-song with the boys of the College *[St. Joseph's Marian Brothers seminary]* when Miss Roberts from HQ arrived with a rumour that North Holland was freed. On top of this in dashed a Father inviting us into the play-ground to hear an announcement on the Dutch radio. The boys were assembled and they willingly acted as interpreters until finally they completely lost control and went hay-wire - a rather infectious proceeding which soon involved Fathers & Relief Workers. Before we were finished we were marching behind the boys who had produced two Netherlands flags and were setting out to spread the news ... a procession about 400 yards long. To try and describe the emotional reactions in words is impossible but with Liberation and not Victory being the theme we joined in to the full and Ramsay and Ian especially went 'to town'. On arrival back here a huge bonfire was lighted and the singing took on renewed gusto and was still going strong when we took a truck into town to pick up Fred and Stan who were just back from Brussels with a load which was being left in the Red Cross Store.

The town was a moving mass of people and the truck had to nose its way through a singing dancing mass of humanity - this was especially dense around a bonfire in the centre of the main crossing. On reaching this it turned out to be the points-policeman's box, plus many other military signs. At Red X HQ we checked up on their arrival and as they were no longer there we tracked them down to the Officers Club where with the Scout drivers they were having supper in an atmosphere rather out of harmony with the lads. Flunkying waiters in evening dress, Orchestra playing and soft lights with deep comfy armchairs plus a heavy atmosphere with a high alcoholic content isn't what they were normally accustomed to but as NAAFI has more or less been tabooed - and at anyrate it's usually difficult to find room there - we make the most of things; and the coffee is good.

The gang picked up the Dutch family with whom we are especially friendly and joined the throng which was now - 11.30 - beginning to scatter somewhat. Just then however the street lights went on and the cheering, singing, and dancing took on renewed life. During the course of our frolics we bumped into some of the Cub-Mistresses who had been here and they put us through the Dutch ring games but we didn't get far at teaching them an Eightsome reel. One girl who was with us and had proved an even livelier wire than most proceeded on the way home in the truck - don't get false ideas as they lived on the route - to give first class impersonations of my accent and crowned the matter with "It's a braw bricht nicht etc."

The older boys have shown quite an interest in IVSP. To further this we have named four of the trucks after Schemes *[ie work-camps, services or projects]* - The Hermitage, Pebmarsh, Lagarde, Shantipur (The Village of Peace, built on a higher level after floods, with Europeans and Indians working together).

The Dutch people are certainly a tidy race and their houses would appeal to you as they offer plenty variety of design and even in the working class area they have no drab streets of Corporation Houses. Up to date I have seen no Dutchman under the 'affluence of incohol' - not even last night when, if ever, they had reasonable excuse.

SNAPSHOTS - TILBURG

Fred Pitkeathly (Unit 4)

Friendship with one youngster, on garden chores - disconcerted by lack of response one day: it was Thursday silence day.

With Stan to Brussels collecting supplies — news of end of war (Europe) - resisted invitation to stay for celebrations to return home to team — every town, village, house, had cheering crowds. Tilburg where MPs directing traffic had central stand - now on fire.

Joined other teams, staff and students in celebratory social & concert - our combined choir under baton of Taffy from Tonypandy helped our contribution.

Suggested to us that our parting gift to budding young missionaries should be - cigarettes.

Letter, 17/5/45, FJM to Alastair.

UNDER MOVEMENT ORDERS

We had been asked to supply transport for a Hungarian Gypsy band and so about 8.15 with a guide I set out to find the encampment and bring Father and four sons along complete with instruments. I'm afraid IVSP have attained rather a reputation for unconventionality and this dance gave further scope, with Ian and Fred turning several of the Dances into adapted Scottish variations. At 1.30 in pitch darkness Ian & I ran them home and managed to find this camp on the way back!

Tuesday morning and still no further news came until about lunch time when the Scouts got orders to move to Amsterdam and the Guides to Rotterdam - & so the combine was broken. It was rather a touching farewell as many members in both teams expressed their regrets very strongly and little did we think we had created such an impression. Not only did the Scouts & Guides leave but Bath & Laundry Units, Dutch Red Cross, and a Red X Hospital team also, leaving only us, a Laundry Unit and half of a Red X Hospital team in the camp. No news came either yesterday or today and so we wonder what we have done to be thus forgotten - or have HQ some special commission for us? This is the opinion of the Major i/c of the camp when he had supper with us last night. Yes! Supper with the Major and it was a most interesting conversation as he was giving us some idea of the set up in Holland where at the moment might is right and the underground virtually in charge of affairs. His attitude to the Collaborationists is very sound and humane and so is that of the camp Kommandant (Dutch) but this doesn't appear to be the case at a nearby camp where Gestapo methods are the rule. The folk in the camp are supposed to be collecting civilian rations and if so the civvy must be hungry as the men here who sweep up behind us on leaving table gobble up the crumbs we leave - and perhaps we sometimes make a mistake and leave big crumbs!

PRESS PROPAGANDA

I was glad to hear of the return of the PoW and perhaps their more honest accounts will do something to counteract this awful bitterness that sections of the Press are creating in the Public mind. The Dutch have suffered, the Displaced Persons have suffered, but in conversation with them I have yet to come across the idiotic bitterness of, say, the Daily Mirror. The foolish utterances of the Editor make me realise more than ever that the spirit of Nazi Germany lives on in minds outwith the German nation. The Scout and Guide teams have also found this absence of bitterness in the Dutch and several of them have toned down as a result of experiences here. Not for a minute do I offer excuse for the fiends at Belsen or Buchenwald but in no way does that condemn 80,000,000 people - or at least what's left after our raids on the large cities.

Letter, 21/5/45, from Bilthoven, FJM to Alastair:

"BRAMHAM'S CIRCUS"

At last we have our job set out before us. We are running a Depot for hospital supplies of special foods which entails considerable transport owing to the wide nature of our field of activity - the whole area latterly occupied by the Germans. All officers from the Col. down have impressed upon us the responsibility of our task and it appears that we have been held back for this job as a result of our work at Tilburg. It's a lovely district of Bearsden type - and when we were led to two large semi-detached houses we again were impressed with the Red X idea of roughing it!

The Burgomaster & Town Clerk are unable to do enough for us and it was with difficulty that we restrained them from giving us all the furniture removed from the houses of collaborators. While they do keep a careful record of all such stuff we don't like the idea of piling the place with other folks' stuff needlessly.

Last night about 6 pm a Despatch Rider came to the door with a letter authorising us to collect 30 tons of goods to start with and so Ramsay and I went to the Depot to fix up transport arrangements. Alas the biggest portion of the goods were already off to somewhere else and so we had to dash up to the Major i/c Civil Affairs to see what was what. He in turn took us in our truck to Netherlands HQ where the Medicine Man in charge turned out to be a Scot. He roped in another Major and they all got down to discussion as to how & where the goods could have gone. Phones went and at last they were located at Rotterdam and we have to await further investigation before we can get ahead.

I have a growing respect for the Army as an organisation as for each mix-up exposed they put through tons of material according to plan. It was a most interesting evening as the Scot knew everything from A to Z and the others kept piling him with questions about conditions here there & elsewhere. The concern shown by these men surprised me and the humanitarian instincts are well & truly roused. *[Major Harvey - the Scot - adopted his own code-name for the Unit's Operation:* 'Bramham's Circus'*]*.

We have been living on field-rations for the past week and so are looking forward to the appearance of bread on the table tomorrow as the sight of Army biscuits doesn't raise any enthusiasm now. It's surprising how varied a menu the girls managed to make out of Bully, Spam, Tinned potatoes and carrots. Yesterday however we got our share of the first fresh meat which has arrived at Utrecht for months and fresh potatoes was also a pleasant addition.

Letter, 28/5/45, FJM to Alastair.

GETTING GOING

Last Monday an RAMC Captain came here with the first list of Hospitals to which we were to deliver the Supplementary Feeding Units mentioned and at 2 am Ramsay, David and I were still working out routes, etc. At 6.30 we were at the Docks (Canal) at Utrecht and loaded up 4 Units (1 Unit is supposed to be enough (light & tempting drinks) for 100 patients for 1 month) which were taken to the Hague for delivery. I was left in charge of HQ here at Bilthoven. After delivery of the Hague consignment they met snags. Theoretically they were to go to Rotterdam and lift supplies there for a further delivery in that town but on arrival they found no one with a knowledge of where the Units were, nor able to give much help. At length after direct enquiries at various Docks they were located and the struggle for authorisation to lift began. It was about 5.30 when they got this and so it was about 9 pm before they left for home. Ramsay and Stan got here about 11, Ian & Fred about 1.30 and David & Douglas about 2.30. All had been lost to varying degrees and the last pair had the added responsibility of a broken down car in tow which kept them back. On Wednesday an early visit from the RAMC Captain with a further list of Rotterdam and Hague Hospitals sent David, Douglas and me off on a truck and Ambulance - leaving our 3-ton, truck and other Ambulance for local delivery as we had an assurance that we would have a lorry lent to us at Rotterdam. I went in to the Officer i/c Civilian Affairs in the Town Hall and found he had left for lunch and was awaiting his assistant - another Lt. Colonel - when a yet bigger 'Big Shot' asked if he could help and ultimately offered to take us down to the Officers Mess to see Lt. Col. Humphries. We had to follow his Staff Car through some of the much bombed areas of the town and it is even worse than West Ham. — In to the Officers Mess where we met Lt. Col. who claimed to know nothing about transport, he passed us to the Major in charge of Transport who then began to squabble with a Capt about the possibility of giving us transport. Things looked bad as with only a 15cwt & Ambulance we could not do much

EXTRA TRANSPORT !

We lunched there and over the meal we got round the obstacle and ultimately got three 6-tonners. We parked our own vehicles and with a boy-Scout as guide on each lorry made for the docks where alas another battle began to get possession of the goods as they claimed our authority had applied only to the Units supplied the previous day. However by 5.30 we got loaded up and away in various directions. The Scout knew his way excellently and the Driver also was a good-guy with plenty of interest to talk about.

It's a long time since I have been so popular as when I went in to arrange delivery of the Unit at the first Hospital. The Sisters and Nurses rushed out of wards and showered thanks on us and perhaps imagining that I was some hero they even sought my autograph. The same story followed at each place and things seemed to have been bordering on the impossible when the first food was dropped by plane. Since then the normal supplies have been coming in but this was the first of the 'tempting' foods - Ovaltine, Bengers, Pearl Barley, etc. - they have seen for ages. (Have I mentioned that 1 Unit is made up of:-

18 cases of milk (48 tins in each case)

4 cases of sugar (6 tins of 7 lb each in each case)

2 cases of coffee (6   do.   do.)

1 case of Pearl Barley, Ovaltine,, Bengers, Cocoa

1 case of Arrowroot, Baking Soda, Cornflour, etc.)

LOCAL CONTACTS

Last night we had two sets of visitors - an English woman and her Dutch husband, and two girls whose mother we are taking to Hospital tomorrow. They sang and played on the Grand Piano which we now have here as the result of a careless remark made to the Town Clerk. Ramsay merely mentioned in conversation that he missed a piano and in about an hour the Town Clerk was back saying we could have one right away and wouldn't take no for an answer. We have to be mighty careful how we say things or along he comes with what we want. Before we knew of this danger Ramsay asked him if it would be possible to get scales to weigh broken packages etc. and he immediately arranged for delivery of two brand new ones.

Taped Recollections Stan Slee (Unit 4)

THE RETURN

There were a lot of Dutch civilians who had been carted off to Germany and put into camps. The Army asked us to help them get some of the survivors who were fit enough back to their homes.

On one occasion I had one elderly woman left in my vehicle because when I'd taken her back to her home it wasn't there: it had been blown up. She was so anxious to get home and see her daughter who had been expecting when she, the mother, had been arrested. Neighbours knew that the daughter and baby had survived the bombing but did not know where they were now. We drove all over the place to friends who might have taken in this girl. No luck. The woman dissolved in tears. She would never see her daughter alive again. How could God who had rescued her so far, do this to her? I sat her in front with me and put a consoling arm round her, then drove slowly out of the village intending to return to the unit with her. Then I saw a woman hanging out clothes, stopped, screwed down the window and said "Do you speak English?". She said yes, as I might have expected.

Then I said "I'm looking for ..." when she saw her mother, you see. She rushed across the lawn, dropped her washing, snatched up the baby from the pram. Meanwhile I was fighting to keep the mother off me; she was trying to crawl through the window. The girl came across, opened the door and hurled herself and baby and the lot on top of us, and we were a sort of rather soggy heap of screaming humanity. I was trying to stop myself crying. It was a great re-union.

ACHIEVING THE IMPOSSIBLE

Another job was to pick up a Dutch patient from one of the villages, a woman who had had an abortion, was seriously ill and had to go to hospital. The doctor came with us to the house. You know how Dutch people make use of every inch of space in their homes - no space wasted on wide staircases - attics occupied. He led us up two steep staircases and then up a sort of ladder to the attic where this woman was, on a bed. We'd left the stretcher downstairs: you could never have used it on these steep narrow stairs. One of us would have to carry her. We'd played about a lot on heavy rescue and demolition in London carting people up and down ladders in our spare time for a bit of fun.. You put somebody over your shoulder in a 'fireman's lift'. But this was going to be the first real 'casualty' I'd ever brought down a ladder. So I demonstrated with Alan [Jessett] how we were going to do it. "Oh no, no, no," said the doctor. We would kill her. We should have to carry her in our arms. You know, I wasn't sure it would be possible. As Alan and I discussed it the patient on the bed said in good English: "Would you do something for me, please?" We nodded. "Would you mind bending down low enough for me to hug you and give you a kiss, because you are the first of my liberators I've seen." After that and our explaining that we were only Red Cross workers, I picked her up - that was all right - Alan went ahead of me below on the ladder to place my feet on the rungs, and the doctor helped me on to it, steadying the top of me as I made my first step. It was an absolute piece of cake! No

trouble at all! Five minutes before I would not have said it was possible. I just carried her straight down - it must have been their confidence in us, and the fact that it just had to be done.

And that sort of thing happened quite a lot. We found we could do more than seemed possible.

Letter, 2/6/45, FJM to Alastair.

GETTING TO KNOW HOLLAND

This has been another hectic week though enjoyable none the less as we have got rid of other 50 Units (25 tons of stuff). On Tuesday morning I got word from the RAMC Captain that the goods had arrived at Utrecht and so I went down to check up and found this to be the case but alas the cases were packed in quantities much too large for our purpose which meant we had to take everything to here (Bilthoven) and break open the cases and take out tins of stuff. On Wednesday Mary and I called at the CA to try and 'borrow' transport as the area for distribution meant long trips to Den Helder, Alkmaar, Purmerend via Amsterdam. Major Milne couldn't help us and suggested we go to Netherlands HQ and tap them. Along we went, swung the car into the Park took a few snappy salutes and then went up to find Major Harvey and his Captain out. I found that the Sgt. in the office was a Hillhead chap and he took us to the RASC section where after spinning our tale to a Major he arranged to 'lay on' (official jargon) 5 six-ton lorries at 8 am. Along they rolled and as everything was ready we didn't take long to load up and get away with each lorry carrying civilian passengers to Amsterdam etc. We are almost running a bus service now and being the only means of getting anywhere we are showered with requests. We had a Dutchman (of whom more later) with us who travelled in the cab and acted guide while Winifred and I made a nest mid the cases in the back. It was fortunate that we were there as on several occasions lads jumped on the back with the object of pilfering. You can guess how they jumped when I popped up.

We received the usual welcomes at the Hospitals and at Purmerend at an RC Hospital the Sisters showered out of wards, rooms, down staircases etc to see the "English Officer". None of them could speak English & so you can guess how I felt but they sent for a Father who came along and saved the situation. He turned out to be of the same Order as St. Joseph's and had heard about us from a Brother who had been up to see him. We were "dragged" into tea and poor Winifred was embarrassed as she walked through the hordes of black clad figures who literally gaped as they had never seen a lady in khaki before. While at tea two girls donned the National Costume which now appears to be worn only in little villages - and each has its own variation and designates whether Catholic or Protestant. Stan & Alan who made the trip to the North West point met the SCF and Scout Teams and both had just received word to move into Germany. We too would have been moving but after a struggle the Medical Auth. have managed to retain us for another fortnight in the hopes that we'll get the supplies to finish this job in that time as they doubt the ability of the Netherlands Red X to do the job. This certainly has put IVSP on the Relief Map as we have heard from various teams that our praises have been sung rather loudly — and all because we have managed to bum [sponge] Army lorries at the right moment and also keep complicated charts which no one but us can understand. Sound policy this last point as it makes the job seem very complicated.

BACK TO IVSP ROOTS

Germany! We don't have the same urge to go there now as we had three weeks ago for various reasons 1) We hear that the no fraternisation order is being strictly enforced and is naturally causing bitterness. 2) That the Displaced Persons camps must be equipped and maintained by the Germans which means practically looting their homes for supplies, and 3) We have landed into a hot-spot of friends here.

For the full significance of the following entry, see "The Long Arm" p.182

On Tuesday of this week a tall, pleasant individual came up to Bruce and I who were working on the vehicles and started to talk to us and we awaited the customary request for 'fags'. His conversation however took another line and he sought information about IVSP. Being in overalls our Service Civil Vol. Int. flash was not visible otherwise his enquiries would have been unnecessary. You will no doubt have jumped to the conclusion — Here was Kees Boeke the International Secy of the Fellowship of Reconciliation who in 1920 called the Conference out of which IVSP originated. You can guess how we all felt, the coincidence amazed us. Since then our nights have been late nights and very valuable also as we now have the pacifist impression of occupation with its resultant hunger, fear & persecution. He has a very interesting family of one son and seven daughters and numerous son-in-laws & friends. Today for instance he sent along a Quaker who worked with Lewis MacLachlan on War Victims Relief during the last war. She lives a short distance away and we intend to go to her place as her children (18 & 16) are anxious to try out their English. She had the usual collection of amazing tales of escape and intrigue especially in relation to helping Jews to escape. Her husband spent 9 months in prison - six in a Concentration camp and the most outstanding point of facts revealed was that the camp guards were former occupants of the camps in Germany who only retained this limited freedom by fulfilling the harsh orders. ... It appears that at first the occupation didn't cause much inconvenience but with the start of the Jewish persecution the Quakers and Pacifists began to operate an underground system of escape, falsification of identity cards etc and carried on at this work until the liberation. They however declined to enter the ranks of the militant Underground which developed on a national basis about a year ago.

DIFFICULT LESSONS

Kees Boeke like the rest of his family has undergone a period of inner conflict that I feel I too would have to face if in a similar position. How far can a pacifist go with the resistance movement? Must one stand apart and live up to high ideals or compromise and assist say a sniper to escape the penalty. Can one abandon truth at will when the lives of friends are at stake?

Returning to the delivery of the letter from St. Joseph's [given by a student in case his family could be contacted]: this made me realise how much modern society accepts the benefits of mail, and transport. When I went to the door the girl who answered took one look and let out a shout, another sister joined her & then their Mother and they danced round the room as they haven't had word for months.

Letter, 9/6/45, FJM to Alastair.

REFRESHMENT

On Sunday afternoon Ian & I went for a woodlands walk with Julia & Theodore (Boeke) and as the scenery was fine & also the company we had an enjoyable period of relaxation — believe it or not it's about the only two and a half hours I have been completely away from Unit work for about three weeks. To do this job thoroughly takes a lot of time but it's by no means irksome and up to date I have enjoyed the state of affairs.

When we got back we found a full house as many other visitors had come along and when at 9 pm we started our evening service about 20 were still here and united. Unless one was in a group the noise was deafening but everyone seemed happy and while Doug, van Gelder [the Dutchman previously mentioned] and Ramsay would be playing on two violins and piano, another group would be back on to Underground adventures, while yet another would be arguing on the possibility of remaining honest — as Julia put it "when one has gazed into a fiery furnace it doesn't seem much to look at a match." ... When we talked of overcoming evil with good in the comfort of a safe home it sounded a lot different from saying the same thing here. ... Kees Boeke was faced with the problem of expelling the Jewish children in order to be permitted to give his type of education to gentile children - this was contrary to his conscience but had he an alternative?

While waiting for Major Wallace on Monday morning his typist got on to this point when she criticised the Underground for branding the Professors as collaborationists. From there we went on to other points which brought out about IVSP ideas, pacifism, future peace etc. and I was sorry to some extent when the Major arrived.

GETTING ON WITH THE ARMY

I can't say I feel overawed by the array of pips and we have the strange position of having no senior officers to concern ourselves with, Cols, Majors & Generals seem to be equally - shall we say charitable to us. I must say that we feel we're wasting our time dealing with mere Lieuts. All round, the Army treat us very well and make things easy for us in many ways but strange to say some of the BRC teams not of our way of thinking have fallen foul of some departments.

On Tuesday when at Red X HQ which is now at the Hague I was speaking to Col. Agnew and Mr. Hogarth (Secy of COBSRA) and they seem to have obtained rather queer ideas about the job we're doing and the methods employed. From being rather dubious about our democratic methods they were swinging round to approval though I can't see it being universally adopted.

SNAPSHOTS - BILTHOVEN

FP

The English lady overcome to hear English spoken in one of our trucks. She spoke to Mary and later contacts heard of life during the occupation - how her son spent 6 months under the floorboards to avoid conscription.

The Boeke family, who provided some female companionship. One entertainment we provided turned out a marathon. When they struck up "We won't go home till morning" at 1 am I felt, after a tiring day, that hospitality must take second place to sleep.

One of the girls was friendly with Prince Bernhard's chauffeur - on his night off he took some of us, with lady friend of course, to the cinema in the Royal car.

The chemist, with whom Douglas found a common interest in music: I discovered Mary Queen of Scots fascinated him - he told me much about her the history books left out.

The young doctor, met through the scabies clinic, who took me to a church service in a schoolroom - they were in the throes of a controversy, leading to a disruption (shades of Scotland 100 years ago) and the dissenters were banished from the Kirk.

When the Mayor came to thank us and presented little badges, the town clerk told me his sister was married to a Scots minister, and had me draw a map to show me where she was, in Perthshire.

On a delivery to a hospital in the north, the expanse of water with only the tops of telephone poles and chimneys showing above.

The doctor in that hospital, isolated through the occupation, still conversing fluently in English.

The welcome given to returning deportees, led by Wilhelmina.

Letter, 24/6/45, FJM to Alastair.

PRE-WAR RECREATION: POST-WAR DEVASTATION - PLUS!

As the Red X HQ is near Scheveningen, Jane [a Dutch nurse] wanted to have a look at the sea so we headed that way to be met by a road block with barbed wire and netting but after some chaff it was moved by a guard and he escorted the ambulance

midst rubble and debris into the remains of beautiful gardens and midst beautiful buildings which bore their scars with dignity. The beach was thick with mines, tank traps, & the concrete gun-emplacements seemed to offer no hope of penetration. Then for home with Ramsay at the wheel and Jane playing rather a fast line. I'm not saying I didn't carry her on a bit but Ramsay twisted the story so much that no one would "deprive" me of taking her to the Hospital tomorrow.

Letter, 1/7/45, FJM to Alastair.

MISSION ACCOMPLISHED - WHAT'S NEXT?

This has been a busy week though very gratifying as we cleared the Docks at Rotterdam three days before we expected and so we have a clean sheet and are ready to move on whenever we get word. The drivers in the end were all anxious to come and stay here overnight and they were like five extra IVSP members. Bert who was the first one to brave the ordeal was a most witty and likeable lad with quite 'Officerish' appearance in fact he was writing in the sitting room one evening when a man came to the door and wanted to speak to the Senior Officer - indicating Bert. You can imagine the chaff his mates made out of this. Our position amused them and when on Wednesday George and I were held up at a Hospital at Amsterdam owing to a pageant at which the Canadians were parading to receive the praise of the populace he laughed at the Colonel's face when I told him we must go through. George contends that no pips less than a Cols would have allowed me to get away with this if I had really been in the army.

After lunch *[on Sunday 1/7/45]* we left the Guides and called at the RASC Garage to collect an ambulance cushion that had been left in one of the lorries and while there I went in to the billets to see if any of the lads were about. Bert was ironing his pants and greeted me with the usual chaff. The looks on the faces of the other occupants of the room expressed surprise and it dawned on Bert that they took me for an officer and thought he was being a bit fresh. I had on my new battle-dress which is a lighter shade of khaki and a good fit which perhaps caused the impression.

SNAPSHOTS - IN TRANSIT CAMP

FP

All the chores performed by women with shorn heads (alleged collaborators) - depressing to see their downcast demeanour.
Lively entertainment by a gypsy ensemble, from Rumania/ Hungary?
The sombre sight of whole towns flattened, in ruins.
Misleading road signs (deliberate!)

THE TRUTH WILL OUT

DUTCH C.O. FINDS THE WAY

Piet Kruithof

We are writing late May, early June 1945. I am working with a relief team of the Dutch Red Cross on the border with Germany, north of Almelo. We are engaged in the repatriation of some of our countrymen who were forced to work in the war-industry of Nazi Germany. I had lived through these years at home in Maastricht, having been lucky enough to have been put to work in Aachen, which meant that we could at least return home by train every evening. We lived under the flight path for the attacks on the Ruhr area, and thus slept uneasily most nights, but at the time I am writing about we had been free for some time: Maastricht was liberated by the Second US Army on September 13th 1944 - the first larger city in the Netherlands to be freed.

I had grown up in a socialist family, where the maxim, coined by Kees Boeke in the early twenties *no man, no woman, no penny for the army*, had always had a good resonance.

As we had lived smack on the border near Aachen until 1936 I had witnessed how week after week the earliest refugees escaping Nazi persecution, mainly for political reasons, came to our house from where they were helped onward to the central aid offices in Amsterdam, which would relocate them either in the Netherlands, or help them to seek exile in other countries like Britain or the USA. From meeting these people, many of them Jewish socialists, I had in my early teens already learned that it was the Nazis rather than the Germans as a whole whom we had to blame for the threat their party threw over Europe. When we were invaded by the German troops in May 1940 I accordingly could not just simply become anti-German, but always spoke up amongst my peers on behalf of 'the other Germans', which did not make my life any easier.

The anti-fascist, anti-militarist tradition in the family caused me much anguish during the following war years and I did quite a bit of reading up on the history of pacifism with the help of books that in our circle of friends, fortunately, were still readily available.

Anyway, when the war ended I was convinced that this should never happen again: Käthe Kollwitz's flaming post-World War 1 protest-poster 'Nie Wieder Krieg' was engraved on my mind, and I was then, twenty years old, determined that I would never let myself be conscripted into the army. But at that particular time we were not sure at all whether the Dutch laws, on the book since 1923, which recognised conscientious objection and alternative service, would be honoured by the government: everything was so very much in turmoil that you really could not be sure of anything at all, and rumours had it that the Dutch authorities in London were planning to conscript an army to be sent as an expeditionary force to the Netherlands East Indies to deal the Japanese a final blow and restore the occupied colonies to H.M.'s rule.

It was in these circumstances that I received a note from Hans Wertheimer, one of the boys I had worked with in Belgium during the preceding winter months but who had not, as I had, joined the Red Cross Aidcorps. How he managed to get this letter through still puzzles me, but in it he told me he had been able to make contact with a unit of relief workers of the British Red Cross who had asked him if he would be willing to come along with them when they moved on into Germany, evidently looking to him to help them out as an interpreter.   They had been put to work in the concentration camp in Neuengamme. He ended the note "Why don't you come and help us here?   We need more people desperately!"   He suggested that I should contact the Headquarters of the British Red Cross in the Netherlands, which he knew to be at Tilburg, and their address: 41 R.C.A.

So I decided to take this up and find out whether I could join the British Red Cross and so find an escape from the threat of conscription.   I was entitled to a day off and used it to set out on my search for 41 R.C.A.!

Public transport was non-existent, but hitchhiking was relatively easy, particularly when you were in uniform, so in my blue Red Cross uniform I managed to get to Tilburg, right across on the other side of the Netherlands in a quite short time, only to find that nobody there knew anything about a Red Cross HQ more than that it might have been there weeks ago, but had moved on. 'Try Utrecht' they said.

At the Town Major's office, 'No Red Cross here, but it seems there is a bath-and-laundry unit in de Bilt.' That was near enough and on I hiked, to find yes, there had been this unit (I later learned it was an FAU team) but as far as anyone knew they were most likely in Nijmegen by now.

I became quite disheartened at this point in mid-afternoon, and felt I'd better give up for the day and return to my base.   But while I walked down the street to the main road, where I had to take a right turn, I happened to look over my left shoulder and by chance saw a blind receding wall totally covered with at least 60-80 military road-signs, and somewhere in the middle a tiny white one with a red cross caught my eye, and the legend 41 R.C.A. Yippie!

I soon enough found a military vehicle to drive me the short distance into Bilthoven, where the sign indicated to turn into a quiet lane and there, in front of a villa, was a sort of abracadabra: Unit 109 IVSP, COBSRA under 41 Red Cross Administration.

Without knowing what it meant, on I went up to the open front door which confirmed my feeling of having arrived at an office of some importance! I knocked on an inside door, expecting to find a room-full of office staff busying away, and was quite taken aback when the 'come in, please' turned out to have come from a man in khaki, whom I had evidently woken up from a cosy afternoon snooze, who then rose with some effort from that incredibly easy-looking chair and said "I'm Douglas Childs. What can I do for you?" Ever so un-English this, altogether, so that I lost all my re-assurance and rather haltingly uttered that I might be wrong in assuming that this was the BRC HQ I so much had hoped to find. "No, that's now in the Hague", Douglas told me. As a matter of fact their team leader, Ramsay Bramham, had gone over there for the day and could be back any moment. Maybe I could wait and talk to him. Or what did I really want to find there so urgently?

Question of conscience that one was. So I rather reluctantly told Douglas my story, about wanting to go and work with the BRC in Germany. "But why would you want to do that? See, we have come from England to help here and I would assume that there will be plenty more work to do by the Dutch Red Cross (pointing at my uniform) after we have gone." So I even more reluctantly told about the rumours of conscription and the East Indies and me not wanting to become a soldier. To which Douglas searchingly asked "so you are a CO then?" and I felt rather sheepish admitting that to a man in khaki who after all had been part of an effort that had delivered us from the heels of the enemy. But upon my "Yes" - said with trepidation (still felt today) - Doug jumped up, pumped my arm and said "but we are all COs here too." At that moment the door opened and I was introduced to Ian Meldrum with the simple recommendation: "Piet is a Dutch CO" and the same kind of warm welcome followed, repeated when Winifred Roberts, David Sainty and Finlay McLaren came in to see whether the tea was ready!

It was then decided that I'd do best to stay and wait for Ramsay to come back - and oh, they were just expecting some people to come in to be treated for scabies and with me speaking

Dutch and probably familiar with the procedure would I like to help out? I found myself with a rubber apron in the garage, which served as a cleaning workshop, doing what I had become quite used to during the preceding months. Ramsay arrived, we had a long talk, it was getting later and the decision was taken by my new friends that it was too late to hitchhike back so I'd better stay for the evening meal, they'd put me up and I could leave first thing in the morning.

Nobody mentioned at that stage that the Boekes were coming over for the meal that evening, so my surprise was great when an hour or so later in filed Kees and Betty, followed by nearly all their offspring and I remember Hans Turksma and Nico de Graan amongst them.

That evening we decided to organise a workcamp on SCI principles (of which I learned a great deal that evening, never having heard of it before) and that is virtually when we started Internationale Vrijwillige Hulpdienst - IVH, later changed to VIA - as the youngest branch on the international tree. Two months later we were at work in our first work camp in Zetten, which Swiss friends helped us to get organised. So, from a series of chance events including another coincidence involving the Boekes the course of my life was set in both Dutch and International SCI, and I was enabled to attend the first international postwar conference 1946 in Brussels, the Easter conference 1947 in Paris and the Askov gathering later that year; and to work on one of the two earliest really international workcamps in Germany (1947, Duisburg and Flensburg). In 1966, after I had started to organise the first workcamps in that part of the world during my work for UNESCO in Bolivia (of which I am still rather proud), the Coordinating Committee for International Workcamp Projects sent me to Buenos Aires to set up a regional office for Latin America. After 35 or more workcamps, many committees, and reunions in Verdun, Hamburg/Neuengamme, Bückeburg, Haarlem and Sweden I rejoice in writing this to realise how many lifelong and precious friendships these events have given me which have enriched my life tremendously.

GERMANY (I)

DISPLACED PERSONS CAMPS IN GERMANY

Our first visitors arrived last Wednesday - Italians, Rumanian, Belgian, French, & Lithuanian, about 350 in all and next day they were joined by 500 Yugoslavs and 45 Czechs. To add to this "League of Nations" we had the twenty German cooks and a cleaning up party of about 30-40 more. We had no incidents and our POWs seemed to be on quite friendly terms with the DPs. Russia not Germany would appear to be the hated nation of all the people we come in contact with here and the small nations look to Britain and France to do something about the "Menace". Even the Yugoslavs who claim to be Communists regard Russia as another grasping Power. You may ask how we found this out but Ian is a great linguist and if they can't speak English, French & German is just as good to him.

The POWs we have here provide a fair cross-section of the population and their background is that of the conscript and not of the ardent volunteer. And what surprises me is the absence of any display of bitterness, insolence and on the other extreme servility.

Human problems are on our doorstep all the time — a Jewish lad of 17 came in with the Yugoslavs who had adopted him on his release from a concentration camp where he had lost both parents & brother. Now however he thought he had travelled far enough with them and as he wasn't anxious to return to Rumania (his homeland) he wondered if he could get to France Britain or America.

Our transport is increasing and we now boast a DKW and an Opel. This increase in transport came to us without us as much as indenting for it and after UNRRA teams have been refused an increase in vehicles. While being classed as an UNRRA team and as such sending our 'Director' to the daily conference the military have already placed us in a different category from the 'Good Time boys'.

We have a regular set of visitors from the Battery & DP Bureau Officers and we have some good laughs at each other. I asked Johnny (the Officer i/c indents) if he had been in London during the Flying bombs - and Douglas butted in with "Don't be silly, he was skulking in France at that time." As their company were over in D + 4 you can imagine how this crack tickled them. Strangely enough it was that Company that swept up Tilburg.

SNAPSHOTS - SALZGITTER

FP

Our first billet - and bed-bugs: Hallendorf. A potential trouble spot - when Italians arrived in force at dinner hut with complaints (vociferous) about state of huts. Calmed down when I showed them my bites (on arm!).

The German cooking staff - hotel manager from Vienna in charge - anticipated friction when a group of Tito's guerillas - fine figures, lush brown hair, bristling moustaches, passed through - mild, friendly men.

Camp leaders - Leon Hoppe, from Auschwitz, dedicated to his camp people, declined to have a meal with us (lest he seemed favoured). Pana Fertig, invited me to a camp wedding. Toast (I suspect) from camp brew, not conducive to driving safely on such damaged roads.

Charity consignments - ladies fashion shoes, hardly suited to muddy camps.

Well meaning lady, come to show camp ladies how to craft waste materials.

Letter, 6/8/45, FJM to Alastair.

COLLEAGUES & PRINCIPLES

I was away from the atmosphere of DP camps all day yesterday *[Sunday]* as we left - 8 of us - at 9.30 to join the Friends Relief Service for a day in the Harz Mountains. The FRS are a great bunch and we had plenty chaff at each other's expense as we lay and sunned. Some discussion took place as to whether we should go bathing or mount another hill and in the end the latter course was adopted and we set out to climb a 2,500 ft 'knoll' which carried an observatory on top. The path up was easy and we had enough wind to argue out what we were going to do about the forced repatriation of Ukrainians and Stateless people to Russia. By the time we had staggered up the tower - very reminiscent of Ibrox Press box - we had decided to send a protest to Col. Agnew of Red X & also our respective HQs. The run home by another route was enjoyable but without further incident though I was extremely sorry not to be able to climb The Brocken - the highest of the Harz ridges - but alas the Russian is there!

The Russian! The name means a very different thing to different people and is causing us much head scratching. The attitude of the DPs who have come from Russia seems to indicate genuine fear. Some claim that not a person who was jammed in a cattle truck and brought to Germany for forced labour was sorry to leave the country from which they had no means of escape. Middleton Murry may be nearer correct in his attitude to Russia than many were willing to credit him with being — but time will tell though in the meantime we don't feel inclined to be parties in forcing people back to what might be punishment for having worked in Germany.

ANOTHER PARTY ...

On Saturday evening we had a late night - first I, with Fred, Alan & Mary went to Wolfenbuttel to pick up two of the Hospital Sisters (Estonian) and took them to the pictures before coming back. On coming home the Poles were running a Dance partly in our honour & so out of decency I joined the others there. They certainly made a fine job of the hall as it was well decorated, and the band wasn't bad. "English Officers" (that's us) were ver r r y popular and it was embarrassing to even look round the room as it was a case of catching eyes all the time — poor David had his beard pulled by one rather attractive piece - and the reactions were most surprising. On the basis of this camp I find a new respect for the Poles as for example their policing of the dance was excellent and when asked to go outside to let in fresh air they moved out orderly. We don't know how much of this is due to the relationship that exists between us and the people here but we feel that the IVSP approach of working manually with the people, and thus trying to solve their problems, has borne fruit to some extent.

...AND WHY

From a first lack of desire to work on their part we now have a barber, a smith, an electrician and several other skilled men working over and above the kitchen staff which are now all Poles except for Francis the POW Chef whom they asked to be retained along with Eric the Medical Orderly. POW and Poles seem to be quite pally and each night before the former leave they are dished out with a pail of soup which is more than they got from us as we felt the DPs might raise a noise. Louis our interpreter is a little devil and no matter how we try to stop him he keeps handing over money for Red X and IVSP. He swears he is not charging for blankets and other stuff we issue and that the contribution is voluntary and without pressure but we have our doubts. He has sound ideas on things in general and we are fortunate in having him here as along with his 'staff' he has removed much weight from our shoulders and we are in fact almost in a position to include more work in our daily routine.

The set-up is becoming more complex however as UNRRA is getting more control and the Red X expect to move out by the end of the year. Strange to say the Army prefer to deal with us and would like to have more of our teams here in preference but UNRRA will be taking over from them also — sometime! There is plenty to do but as things stand we may not be here as long as we expected and the chance of other teams coming out is not at all likely. It would be a laugh if we went home and I was sent back to Forestry! The future! What lies ahead? Your guess is as good as mine but one thing I am better armed to face that future than I was a year ago at this time. *[Finlay became Chief Probation Officer of Northumbria Probation Service and founder Chairman of the Prince's Trust Committee for the North East].*

SNAPSHOTS - GEBHARDSHAGEN

FP

Billeted in villa, with German domestics - Helmut (cook), two female helpers (Ruth? ...)

Now we're into administration - responsible for visiting camps, problems and solutions, welfare supplies, encouraging camp staffs.

Contacts with UNRRA American who demonstrated how to throw dice (think he called it the Crap game).

Ramsay & self played for local Mil Gov v Army team.

SNAPSHOTS - BREMKE

Work now with Germans returning from East.
Gasthof Jütte - haunt of Göttingen students pre-war - Mutter Jütte and family took care of all domestic needs - home from home?
Got to know Holtermann family - Dr., wife, two sons, daughter - Horst, Dieter, Anneliese - all to take part in future IVSP activities.
Football match with village team - policeman's boot put me out

of action for a month - with the ski-ing season imminent.

Party for village children - Ramsay doing his Santa act.

Heart-rending scenes on daily trek from railhead on Russian side to Friedland station and transit camp - 4 km (?): transport "nur für Alte, Kinder und Kranke."

Boy of 14 pushing Aunt in wheelchair (dead)!

Every kind of hand-hauled transport with all worldly possessions. Students helping.

Red Cross Nurses - Liselotte and Gisela (the nightingale).

Camp in farm buildings - birth in a stable on Christmas eve.

Mud, and more mud.

Bremke below Gleichen and Eschenberg

WORK REPORT - Week ending 23/11/45, FJM:

REFUGEE TRANSIT CAMP - FRIEDLAND

While we developed along other lines the main activity of the week has centred around Besenhausen where our transport service has been extended to occupy six of us from 9 am until we get the needy cases off the road - usually about 3 pm. The daily average remains about the 5,000 mark with a slightly greater percentage of unfit people. We have tried to arrange entry into the Russian zone to go to Heiligenstadt to pick up cases there but on the first morning our Ambulances were turned back because official approval had not come through.

As a result of a phone message from Miss Roberts (COBSRA Liaison Officer with BRCS at HQ5) we found that we are attached to 229 P Det. though this will not interfere with the work we are doing meantime. As a courtesy visit and to make direct contact David visited Hannover and while being unfortunate in finding neither Major Harvey nor his assistant at home he saw the German Red Cross who have promised to let us have a field-kitchen and thermos containers.

The above mentioned Major Harvey knows IVSP of old as he met the members of Unit 3 who went to the South coast to assist with French refugees and we operated under him in Holland.

Stan accompanied David to Hannover and at a Vehicle dump managed to get the promise of supplies of spares - notwithstanding sign-posting to the effect "No bloody spares available". He intends to return on Monday to prove his reputation as a scrounger.

Letter, 2/12/45, FJM to Alastair:

The reason why people leave their homes is another unconfirmed theory, but at the moment about 50% are refugees from Sudetenland, Poland, etc, and the others, evacuees being ordered to return to the area they left at the time of the bombing.

Among those who came over the frontier 'unofficially' was the Prince of Sachsen-Weimar (nephew of the Queen Mother).

He was accompanied by his wife, child & retainer and wanted us to give him a lift to Göttingen where he wished to see Mil. Gov. as he claimed that his Mother & Sister had been taken East by the Russians. We gave them a seat and then graciously helped them on to the 5 o'clock bus — despite Ian's protest that they had not been deloused.

Letter, 15/12/45, FJM to Alastair.

WINTER CONDITIONS

We have had our spell of winter weather with 15° of frost over two or three days, snow fell intermittently and a partial thaw made the roads in very dangerous state & just to complicate things the brakes of the lorry gave out when I was carrying a load of old people and prams, and for the remainder of the way it was a case of gear changing all the time with bottom gear bringing one down to about 5 mph but never dead stop.   All ended up OK and for this a good horn had to be thanked at times.

The thaw with a day of blustery sleet & rain was miserable and the evacuees & refugees had a miserable time — not to mention us as Alan came in with his rubber boots full of water which had dripped off his coat. I escaped the worst of the day as I was on late Ambulance duty and spent the morning sorting clothing here. It was bad enough as it was, with the gale blowing the Ambulance from side to side of the road and the rain coming in at unexpected places.

We made our first call at The Rohns, a new emergency hospital that has been opened *[in a Göttingen hotel]* and the sight rather shook me even after what we have seen in the past weeks.   A large room which was previously a dance hall now contains about 150 beds - head touching head with about 18" between the feet.   The patients were lying in their own clothes with a single blanket and I leave you to imagine the stench which even sulphur candles failed to smother.   A number of G. Red X staff seemed to be making an attempt to make the people comfortable but it seemed an impossible task under the circumstances - and conditions are not likely to improve as the daily trek seems to contain more & more "fragile" cases. It is certainly not going to be a pleasant Christmas for many but the kids have a surprising way of making light of troubles. Last night when in a hut looking for luggage belonging to a sick woman I found the Nissen full of people & baggage and while some were curled up on the floor trying to sleep, with others hunched on bundles of clothing etc three little nippers were busy making harvest pleats with the straw on the floor.

PATIENCE GIVES OUT

If epidemic breaks out this winter - well least said is best as the means of spreading it are in every hut & shelter to say nothing of the trains which are so packed that some people travel on the buffers and steps. And despite all this the Guides International Service are holding up the Canteen Section until they discuss the question of working with the Germans - if they are not careful they may have deaths on their conscience as even the small amount of coffee we can hand out brings many people round. The Guides in the field are as wild about the hold up as we are but with the well fed Lady Muck & her type on the Committee at home what can one expect. I fear I will not be too tolerant with their type once I get home.

GENERALS GALORE

Another General called upon us - General Martin, War Correspondent for the Daily Telegraph. When Dave met Major Oldham on Wed. he asked if the General had called and David said he knew nothing about him. Oldham in rather a hurt voice said he had heard he was coming to visit the Red Cross Section at Bremke and thought he was another personal friend like General Lindsay. He turned up next morning and by his conversation it was obvious that the Col had primed him in IVSP History as he knew about our reunions at Bilthoven.

SNAPSHOTS - CONTACTS

DLS
News for the YMCA

Bruce and I were invited to meet the President of the German YMCA in a house in Göttingen. We had a long and interesting conversation during which the President asked how many C.O.s there were in Britain. 60,000, Bruce answered. "Sechzig tausend!" he exclaimed, "Erstaunlich! Now I understand how Britain won the war!"

A Medical Emergency

We received a request to deliver some Units of Penicillin from Army Medical HQ to a hospital to the North West where a German doctor was critically ill with some kind of septicaemia. Presumably using our services bypassed all the red tape. Douglas and I set off in the Adler, collected the package in the middle of the night and after some fast winter driving by Douglas delivered it safely into the hands of the medical staff at the hospital. They presented us with an effusively grateful receipt for, I think, 400,000 Oxford Units, conferring undeservedly on each of us in that document the title Dr. Med.

Letter, 22/12/45, FJM to Alastair.

ONE UP ON THE ARMY

I am on holiday today though most of us are virtually in that state as owing to the Russians not countering the original arrangement to close the frontier over Christmas people have not been coming over - only about 1500 today & 1800 yesterday. This break is giving the new camp a chance to get straightened up and the roads repaired, drains dug and such jobs done. The hospital was the last section to move in and this was largely due to the REs not constructing a ramp for us - the steps were impossible for the old and sick.

It rather shook the Army when Ramsay & Ian along with four POWs set about the job and by biting the ear of a bulldozer operator they had the job done in two days - this included a turning point for vehicles. This was originally intended as the exit only but the entrance will not take heavy vehicles as the original road surface is now 4ft under the surface.

All was going well until a rather cocky RTO came marching along to me demanding to know what the Ambulances were doing there & he didn't seem amused when I meekly replied that they were unloading people. He blustered and wanted to know if we didn't know that this was an exit only and as he was in charge of the Railway area we must not enter that way. His manner was so ridiculous, and we had been hashing to get the old people out of the rain which didn't make me too cherubic, & so I waxed rather sarcastic and wanted to know if he had any parachutes and we would land them from the air. He still was not amused & some of his men didn't help as they saw humour in the situation. In the end in face of a watertight argument he fell back on the statement "I'm obeying 30 Corps orders" to which I replied that he no doubt found that a lot easier than using his common sense. Finally I told him to see the Major and in the meantime we would carry on as we were doing - & we still are which would seem to indicate that our first brush with authority has gone OK. Thank goodness we have 'Officer Status' - and friends in 'high places' if the worst comes to the worst.

REINFORCEMENTS

We are increasing Red Cross strength by three Guides & their canteen joining us on Jan. 1st or thereabouts. It is the Canteen Section that was at Tilburg with us, and whom we have met on various occasions since. They are a crazy trio and not typical 'Guides' if you know what I mean. It took them a bit of doing to get permission to come to work with Germans as the Chairman of the Guides feels rather strongly on the point that the money was collected to help the Allies. After a lot of persuasion however they got her to visit us before she returned to England and Dave gave her the 'dope' to such an extent that she has agreed their coming for a month's trial to see if they are really needed.

Letter, 30/12/45, FJM to Alastair.

MORE PARTIES

Stan & I are going up to spend our 72 hr leave with the new Unit near Hamburg. I expect you will have heard that Unit 5 has so enhanced our reputation that Red X HQ have pressed for another team which is in course of formation. ...

Fröhliche
Weihnachten

/SP Christmas card designed by Alan Jessett

Mention of parties makes me feel tired - we had our German guests on Christmas day, Football & Tea with the POW workers from the Camp on Boxing Day and a party for the 150 village kids on top of that. They were all excellent fun and this Christmas stands out in my memory. It really started on Christmas Eve when in our absence at a Carol Service a basket of gifts was placed at the foot of our Christmas tree - then on top of this a youngster came in dressed as Santa Claus and distributed gifts from the Staff at Bremke. For the rest of the evening we sang carols and about 11 pm four of us sat down to play Bridge & carried on till almost 2 am. On Christmas day we had a hectic time helping the Staff get the dinner of Turkey & Goose ready with the usual accessories and finally at 4.30 Doug set off with an Ambulance for Göttingen to pick up some guests while I went to Besenhausen to pick up Nurses. The company mixed exceptionally well and the meal was a rollicking affair with "Ginger" the Mil Gov interpreter keeping things going when the language raised difficulties. Ian who had arranged the tables had fixed things well so that I had English speakers at hand. Ginger was telling us that the Officers at Mil Gov hadn't asked us to their party because they thought we were against amusements of all kinds and went on to say she had expected a quiet evening with discussions on art or literature. She was not given long to change her mind as she had arrived to find a free-for-all going on under the mistletoe. Finally as usual the party had to end and when returning the Nurses and Lagerleiter (Big Shot) to Friedland Stan asked Erasmus where he had been last Christmas and he went on to tell about their experiences in East Prussia where he was Chief of Staff of the German Commandos. Finally we agreed that it was a pleasant change in circumstances and as none of us had changed it seemed nonsensical that we had allowed outside factors to govern our finer instincts. All this frivolity has been possible as the movement of refugees has been stopped over this period.

Letter, 7/1/46, FJM to Alastair.

HOGMANAY ADVENTURES

Hogmanay was as successful as I have been able to recall. Ian, Fred, Dave & I turned up for dinner wearing tartan ties. Shortly after midnight we (Fred, Ramsay, Ian & I) went first-footing and found that the Germans have the right ideas on the subject as even at 4.30 am when we came back all the lights were not out. Most of the time was spent at the house of the Dr. where most of them are English speakers with a son and daughter of about our age. The daughter, when she saw our ties dashed from the room & returned in a tartan dress. Anneliese is interpreter to Bremke and a very good one at that - she is also a useful person to know as she arranges for a supply of horses for us riding on our days off.

As there was a Dance starting at 3 pm *[1/1/46]* the pitch for the match which had been arranged against the POW was lined with Germans who stayed on to watch instead of going in to the start of the dance. We were winning 6-3 when Fred got a bad kick in the shin and with his departure we lost our large lead. Ramsay in a great solo effort scored another goal just on time and in company with the opposition we went in for tea.

Not only Fred's shin upset our "Sisters" but David who had gone to Friedland in the morning had not returned and no message had been received from him. When Marian was on the point of putting through a series of calls to all known contacts the phone rang & David asked for someone to come down & collect him at Besenhausen.

The story has caused us much amusement ever since. He found himself with time to spare and went in search of the stone which marked the junction of the American & Russian Zones. Alas he found himself in Russian hands and he was walked to Arenshausen where he had to wait while they went up step by step until someone would take the responsibility of granting his release. During his wait a loaf, sausage and a bottle of schnapps were presented to him. The Russians wouldn't take no for an answer and they further insisted that he scoffed the glass. To cut a long story short Dave made his way back to the frontier under his own shaky power. As Dave had been upheld as the paragon of virtue to the wayward Scots (Ian Fred & Ramsay - the latter by co-option) who had reached the cheery stage overnight the joke was all the more humorous.

Recollection of the Victim

RUSSIAN ARREST

Snow lay round about, deep and crisp and even. I parked the car near to where I expected to find the marker stone (which was more or less bang in the middle of Germany - hence the interest) and set off to look. Finding a landmark like a stone pillar should have been easy, but it was neither so even nor so easy as all that, because wherever the pillar was it too would be white. As I looked round in the area where I thought it should have been I heard shouting and about 100 yards to the east two or three Russian soldiers holding rifles were indicating that I should join them. So I did, along with one or two other unfortunates. So far as I remember, we did not have to walk far before we reached Arenshausen, the station of which I knew from visits to it with an Ambulance. Where the other arrestees went I don't know but I was taken to the company HQ (a house in the main street)where I was offered a seat, and a bright and friendly young Lieutenant engaged me in such conversation as could be conducted in pidgin German. Not a lot of explanation was necessary, but I was informed that wheels were turning and as soon as an adequately qualified Officer could be contacted I would be released.

I suppose I was in the Guard Room, and one or two privates moved in and out. I had probably seen them before on guard duty at the frontier, where these 18-year-olds (by their appearance) took great interest in the vehicles and our watches, patting the former and examining the latter without being either importunate or belligerent. I seemed to be regarded as either a guest or a visitor rather than an object of suspicion, and the Lieutenant, who popped in frequently to report progress, on one of his appearances asked me whether, if one of them had walked into the British Zone he would have been arrested. I said I didn't think so, and he said that was what he thought, and he considered it quite wrong that I should have been, as we were allies. This was a golden opportunity to enter into the origins, ideals and practices of SCI, but (a) I thought it was sufficiently interesting that he should have expressed such forthright and soundly-based opinions and (b) there was not the faintest possibility that I could have found the pidgin with which to express such ideas. So I smiled and agreed with him, without trying to tell him that I wasn't a soldier but a pacifist. He might well have been interested.

One of the privates brought in my lunch - a piece of rye bread, a very greasy sausage and a half-litre glass of schnapps. The Lieutenant came with it and wished me a good appetite, but that was hardly sufficient. The black bread was fine (I could have dealt with a bigger bit), but how was I going to cope with greasy sausage and schnapps? If I couldn't explain pacifism, there was even less chance of a meeting of minds on teetotalism; nor would it be politic to broach the matter. There was only one course open - eat as big a bit of sausage as I could manage, along with the smallest portion of bread which would help it down, and follow that with a sip of schnapps of a size nicely calculated to exhaust all the liquid at the same time as its blotting paper. I was under interested observation, but it's unlikely that any of that array realised that my daintiness masked a profound struggle, or with what relief I at last emptied the glass.

After an hour or two the Lieutenant announced with pride and joy that a senior Officer had been contacted and that I was free to go, and I would be escorted to the frontier by a private, who then appeared, something over 5' tall. I decided to put my best foot forward and marched up the hill to the frontier post at full speed, having the satisfaction of making my escort trot slightly to my rear. All which is truth.

Letter, 3/2/46, FJM to his family:
We had a visit the other day from the Major with whom we worked in Holland and who is now head of Public Health for this area. It was like meeting an old pal and as we went over certain incidents we discovered that along with others he was responsible for the lighting of the Police box in Tilburg the Night of Liberation.

This is a very woolly effort but two members of the FAU have come in to discuss the future of German Welfare and I should really be giving them some attention.

Letter, 10/2/46, FJM to Alastair:

VLOTHO HQ

I am just back, after leaving here on Wed. morning to take Ramsay & Fred to the staging point en route for home leave. I spent the night at the Guides and went on to Vlotho on Thursday morning to attend a FAU Conference in the afternoon. The conference went with a bang and it was not a "yes man" affair as quite a few had things to say against the FAU closing down in June. The Colonel asked me to stay over another day for another conference and I had a pleasant evening hanging about HQ where we have surprisingly large connections and I ended up supping coffee with the Late-duty Officer who was the chirpy typist that Ramsay & I pulled down a peg in

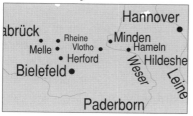

Holland.She was saying that it puzzles her why the Col should fall on the neck of IVSP when we call at HQ.

Next morning Basil, Douglas (FRS) and I went out beyond Minden to see Pastor Mensching who is reorganising the International Fellowship of Reconciliation. He was a great character and despite the unsettled state of things in Germany he is hopeful of getting things going. We got him onto his 1933-1945 adventures and they restored one's faith to realise how a conviction can carry one through such a period.

Letter, 17/2/46, FJM to his family:

REFLECTIONS AT A PARTY

We had a visit from Reg Champ and Ewart Stickings who came here on their 72 hrs leave from Berlin. We enjoyed their visit and Ewart made the most of it when he accompanied several of us to a Fancy Dress Carnival given by the Doctor's family in a large house nearby which is alleged to be haunted. To overcome the curfew regulations the affair started just before the fatal hour and carried on until it was lifted at 4.30 am. The guests came from all the big houses around. During the evening Anneliese the hostess told me that one family had left on our arrival and despite my expression of regret she remained amused as it had been a source of discussion as to what their reaction would be. I did not get it clear what the actual objection to the 'Englander' might be but none the less I had rather a sneaking admiration for their line of conduct as it is more in line with what I should have imagined would have happened in Britain. Not that it is necessarily correct because of that but because I feel that at times the display of friendship is superficial and aimed at personal favour. In conversation it caused no end of surprise that we had the possibility of refusing war service as they automatically thought conscription had put an end to that.

Our favourite Guide has gone home as the result of straight-laced priggishness. The ins and outs of the story don't matter as she was asked to resign and has gone but now comes the climax that has us in howls of suppressed laughter.

A Guide vehicle was going to Holland and Dougie enrolled as Driver's-mate and they got well and truly pied up in the flooding. On one occasion they had travelled 250 miles in an attempt to find a bridge and ultimately arrived in Nijmegen to find that accommodation was almost impossible. At last they found a house that said in a mixture of German-Dutch-French-English that they would be accommodated and they washed and dined. Then Dougie made a discovery - they had only one room between them. However neither felt in a fit state to worry and they made some mutual arrangement about retiring and rising. When they ultimately got to Vlotho they found a degree of concern amongst one new team that in the emergency accommodation there the screening left something to be desired. To which Dougie replied with feeling "You will soon get used to things like that." Very funny and we know the Guides in general would share the joke, but what would the Commissioners say?

SNAPSHOT - NEAR MISS

DLS

In the hardest period of the winter of 1945/6, when the roads were hard-packed snow, Ian and I returned from Vlotho to Bremke in the Adler, Ian driving. At the approach to a main road a car in front of us ran over a jettisoned can which caught in the undercarriage and caused the car to slide all over the place. Ian was forced to brake and the Adler then proceeded in a steady skid towards the main road which rose in a significant slope to a high point on our right. At that moment there appeared at the top of the slope the first of a convoy of American Army 10-tonners, driven, as much of Transport Command was, by black Americans who had a reputation for stopping for nothing (though on those roads there wasn't a lot any driver could do). "Hell!" said Ian, trying every way to get the car under control, but it sailed gracefully on, sidling slowly across the road as the first of the trucks roared down on us. Surprisingly, my only reaction was interest in the situation, trying to guess whether our momentum would take us past the thundering monster. It did, just. The off front wing of the truck brushed our off rear wheel-arch and pushed us gently on to the verge, facing the way we wanted to go. All we had to do was pull the arch up with our hands to clear the tyre and head for home.

Letter, 24/2/46, FJM to his family:

INTERNATIONAL RELATIONS

Feeling gloriously tired and just a little sleepy after a day trying to become a skier. Half the fun of course is in watching the other guy though in the case of Fritz it is not amusing but a treat. He was trained in Norway where he was stationed when Germany collapsed and for some time he was a POW there. He liked the Norwegian people very much despite the fact that they did not like the Germans in the mass. Fritz is one of the Jütte family and a very likeable lad and on the way home he was telling me of the type of pep talks they were given to lead them to hate the British. As Fritz said, "Propaganda is dangerous when it is proved untrue."

Fred & Ramsay have just returned from leave. We were getting a bit alarmed about their return as both of them were down for the opening of the IVSP Scheme at Friedland which takes place tomorrow. Marian who is acting 'Sister' had things well in hand even to the extent of persuading the Army to lend us 13 pairs of rubber boots for the Volunteers. The scheme is being watched by 'officialdom' and on the result of this experiment further efforts may be made to introduce German youth into the realm of voluntary community service. Even the Mil Gov Officer who has come to Göttingen to 'clean up' the University had heard of it previous to my mentioning it to him when I called with an FRS girl on other business. *(See p 184)*

From PREFACE TO JOURNAL

David L Sainty, Senior Representative

The first international work-camp in NW Europe after the war (but with only two nationalities [three if you're a Scottish Nationalist] - British and German) had been organised at Friedland, Kreis Göttingen. Flash-forward to Glasgow, early 1948 - a small re-union. In the course of conversation, and presumably à propos of something which had been said, Finlay, with the hearty laugh which was always breaking out, threw into the pool "You were a bit of a dictator once, Dave!" This was surprising, and I asked what he meant. He reminded me of the team meeting at Bremke in about November 1945 when the team was having its weekly discussion of the work at Friedland Refugee Camp, and the various contacts there. These included Catholic and Lutheran relief agencies, German Red Cross, and a number of students (male, ex-service) from various faculties of Göttingen University, mostly Law, Medicine and Divinity, who were all mucking in to help. [The colloquialism is appropriate - mud was an early feature of the camp]. Ramsay Bramham suggested that there was the possibility of organising a traditional work-camp to erect further Nissen huts which were badly needed to cope with growing numbers of refugees, shortly to be further augmented by "Operation Swallow" - the removal from the parts of eastern Germany handed back to Poland of all Germans living there. There was a long discussion about this, three members of the team opposing the suggestion on perfectly legitimate and reasonable grounds, mainly that that wasn't what we were there for as a Relief Section of COBSRA. As Finlay noted, I as team leader brought the discussion to a sudden stop by saying, according to his recollection, "Well, that's what's going to happen." The sequel was reported by Derek Edwards in the following paragraphs:

"When David Sainty told the London office that Colonel Alan Andrews of the Army Education Corps (whose second-in-command, an RAF Officer, Robert Rayne, was an IVSP member) had seen the 'unofficial' Friedland work-camp and was intending to call on us in London to discuss the possibility of setting up SCI services in Germany we awaited his visit with eagerness.

"He told us that one of the objectives of his Department was to find ways of demonstrating to young Germans (who had spent their formative years under a dictatorship) democracy in practice. Having seen Friedland he had come to the conclusion that there could be no better way of doing this than by letting them take part in international work-camps.

"He suggested that IVSP should ask for formal permission from the Minister for German Affairs (Frank Bellenger MP) to organise 5 international work-camps in the British Zone that summer. He said that possibly 'with luck' the Minister before making a decision might ask for his advice. It seemed to us a long shot but long shots do sometimes come off and this one did: permission was forthcoming.

"All the countries where SCI had contacts were asked to select volunteers to take part in these camps and 260 volunteers from different countries and from Germany worked together on various projects.

"It was said that the volunteers taking part in these camps were the first 'unofficial' civilians allowed into Germany after the war and when the next year German volunteers were allowed to take part in SCI services in other countries these were the first German civilians allowed out of Germany. This may or may not be true but it was true that all the volunteers taking part in this international voluntary service for peace had their travel costs met by the War Office!"

Several of the Göttingen volunteers at Friedland took leading parts later that year or early in 1947 in establishing the German Branch, notably Hans Temme, a distinguished orthopaedic surgeon, who became its first Chairman after Heinrich Carstens; his friend in Hannover Adolf Meyer, a social worker; Gerhard Meyer, University Librarian at Hamburg; Joachim Frege; Harald von Majewski; Horst Holtermann and his sister Anneliese Ehrhardt. Anneliese was one of the core group, with Marian Girling, Fred Pitkeathly and Ramsay Bramham, the team leader, of the Friedland work-camp. She gave full-time voluntary help in the organising of the first camps and was active in the new Branch and associated work for many years.

FRIEDLAND 1946*

FP

Ramsay, steeped as he was in IVSP ideals, was the obvious choice for leader, Marian to organise the domestic side, and I welcomed the opportunity for practical involvement at a time of uncertainty. A decision I would never regret, particularly when I later learned that so many of the student volunteers took part in establishing a German branch of SCI and subsequent workcamps.

At this point I'd better confess that the recall of names gives me difficulty. For one thing we were on first name terms and over the 4 weeks there would be over 40 students. Each week there was a change of personnel from different faculties. Those who come to mind (often with mental pictures) are Hans, Adolf, Gerhard, Joachim, Harald, Horst, Dieter, Paul, Claus. There were those who were attracted by the idea of service, who were susceptible to Ramsay's ideas, and others, more cynical or by whose background more resistant, but possibly who welcomed a prospect of enhanced rations when German levels were low. They qualified for heavy workers' extras and these plus our generous Army rations made an adequate if basic diet which Marian and her helpers made the most of. I even developed a liking for the black rye bread, heavy but filling - in the Scots phrase "Hunger's good kitchen".

Marian's helpers were Anneliese and Lieselotte, and her organising abilities must have impressed the Germans, although the rota for domestic duties was a culture shock. Here the adaptability, if not the expertise, of their British companions no doubt helped.

On the job, it was hard work in cold, unpleasant conditions. I was with the gang all the time, and have never worked with a harder working or more cheerful group. The initial erection of Nissen huts may be straightforward, but when these have been dismantled and transported, re-erection can pose problems. I was constantly appreciative of the ingenuity shown by my companions.

*Cf Francavilla, p 70

An amusing sidelight occurred when I enquired the reason for an outburst of hilarity. It appeared that a discussion among passing camp-workers was centred on a khaki uniform in a German work force — consensus: "A British soldier serving out his punishment." I'm not sure if this was the reason that the Camp commandant passed me without recognition, looking very business-like with his briefcase. Ramsay enlightened me: it held his *mahlzeit* (Scots "midser").

My knowledge of German was rudimentary, and I lacked Ramsay's confidence, who started from as low a base. The handicap proved less and less as many of the students' English was very good, and they were sympathetic to my faltering attempts. I found too I was following discussions at table and in the evening, when Ramsay ensured our principles were aired. Not all the students participated - a group of Lutherans preferred conducting revival meetings in the camp - with a three-piece band to entertain.

On one occasion I was involved in a discussion with them when racism came up. I was asked "Do you really think a coloured man is your equal?" My reply: "I think the nearest to a Christ-like figure today is an Indian, Gandhi". The look of incomprehension stifled any response.

We had lighter moments - a dance in the village hall, when Unit members and other connections joined in - I remember Ian demonstrating a Highland Schottische - there were visits to Göttingen theatre where we enjoyed opera (Verdi), theatre (Shakespeare) and symphony (Mendelssohn). I've no idea who paid. On Sundays we enjoyed walks in the forest.

For me it was a rewarding experience and I think just possibly a real contribution to the P that IVS had in the shoulder badge I wore, as well as justifying the "pick and shovel" emblem.

DIARY of the IVSP SERVICE
at the Refugee Transit Camp,
FRIEDLAND

(Transcript from the original rough draft in which a different
participant made a handwritten report of each day.
Translated from the German by DLS)

The first entry was written less than 10 months after the German
surrender. Several of the volunteers wore bits of army uniform
(having little or nothing else) - a few were in the black breeches
and jackboots of Panzer or similar regiments).

Monday 25.2.46 Today 12 students, including one girl, arrived at the
Refugee Camp. At 8.45 am Günter K (Caesar), Adolf D (Sani), Paul,
Wolff, Rolf and Gerhardt arrived in a lorry from Göttingen and were
received by Ramsay, Fred, Marian and Joachim [Frege]. The team's
practice of the familiar 'Du' and first names was established right away
and after an ample and satisfying breakfast we went to deal with the
huts. Blankets and working tools were provided: we each had a bed,
chair, rubber boots and waterproof coats marked with a number.
Construction of a toilet with three seats was begun and the sleeping,
stores and kitchen hut, serving at the same time as living and dining
room was made comfortable. Shortly before the midday meal, which
was again very plentiful, Anneliese and Horst arrived, having been held
up by a car breakdown. After the meal came Günter (M) and Heinz,
who had missed the lorry, and Joachim (St). In the afternoon work
went on on the hut and coal and wood were collected. After a tasty
dinner of potatoes, noodles and beef, we sat agreeably round the stove
with songs, accordion- and violin- playing and conversation.

Tuesday, 26.2.46 The first night on round straw mattresses awoke
forcible memories of past times and prevented our getting to sleep on the
hard boards. The newly delivered blankets smelt strongly of DDT, which

on the one hand eased our minds and on the other disturbed our sleep. For the first time we were woken at 6.45, an unusually early rise for a student. Then the temperature in the hut was unusually cold: getting up was no easy matter and we complained forcibly to the kitchen-roster who had carelessly overslept so that the stove hadn't heated up. As getting up was therefore a right hesitant affair we were all late for breakfast. Two minutes after starting time we were not yet outside, but we got to the work place and with German foremen and some Ukrainians we started on the hut-building. At first it was mighty cold but we got stuck in and our enthusiastic activity warmed us and we built a new hut in shorter time than the same number of Ukrainians. When we got back somewhat tired from the unaccustomed work and lots of fresh air, we were amazed at the magnificent culinary marvels conjured up before our eyes on the table. Anneliese had luckily for us accomplished this magic, getting our eatables without ration cards. Then in the afternoon, very late and unshaven after a long train journey, arrived Hans [Temme] and Adolf [Meyer]. They too were amazed. In the evening we had a very interesting visit. Ramsay's cousin came from the Berlin IVSP team, giving us a detailed account of his work and the living conditions there. We listened intently and learned a great deal about the idea of IVSP.

Wednesday 27.2.46 *Oh! Hasten the day when we don't have to get up at 6.45! This morning, Marian yelled "Up you get!" as a morning joke: well, no, that doesn't sound right, but to make sure we were awake she pulled our legs good and proper - nasty!! This is Anneliese's birthday! Being a gentleman, I don't know how many springs she has adorned: there's talk of a lot of birthday cakes!*

We so worked today, right from the start, that I think at least 3 huts were ready together. But to be sure, the highest merit is accorded by the concentrated hostility of our high-ups - oh, ay, we all know the procedures!

The evening was spent at the theatre in Göttingen: dress - rollneck sweater and skipants. What would AH [Der Führer - who else?] have said? We saw What You Will, and note, that between As You Like It and What You Will there's a great difference, for one is in a wood and the other at the seaside (courtesy of Fred). For the rest, the performance was very nice, especially Hedi Reich!

On the way back, 8 years' training in Wehrmacht tanks paid off when our truck stopped, as we naturally saw at once, because of distributor failure. Rather late, we eventually arrived at Friedland, where Anneliese, mourning our absence, put new life in our chilled spirits with the passionately-longed-for cakes and biscuits. So we celebrated until midnight the end of Anneliese's birthday and the beginning of Adolf Meyer's.

Thursday, 28.2.46 *We have with great fervour adopted the habit of counting the days not by hours but by mealtimes which we look forward to, and so I can start today's report: We got ourselves up (from our one or two blankets) for "Breakfast". But at that time probably no one would call it to mind, as had already been clear at 6.45 - and anyway we only unwillingly get accustomed to it. What actually follows is just a race to the table. Here we can renew our long faded acquaintance with transoceanic and oriental fruits - oranges and bananas, and in a combined choir we wished our Atchen [Adolf Meyer] "a happy birthday". Then off to the hut - the second, which is now nearly complete. We couldn't get started on No. 3 because the timber framing wasn't there yet. So some of us could work on finicky detail: the others sang with deep bass voices wild slave-songs from the Palace Roof (from 'Cuban Black Uprising' the theme degenerated into related kinds of creativity of a later date!). If the Hannover Courier could have heard it!*

During and after the second breakfast a gentleman asked permission to film. He did this with great pomposity (slowly did our 'Society for Political Mission' become known to us). He wanted pictures of us actually working, and as there was nothing useful to do we pretended. All wilted in resignation with handtools at the ready while continually he brandished his viewfinder. He called this setting up: to us with memories it was pantomime.

He who would know the lunch these days must look into the cookhouse set-up. So far as he is in some measure proof against attacks on the palate I can recommend it. For the afternoon I was deputed by the inside-service (painful expression!) to make up a programme for the evening. The abundance of my inspiration did not fit easily into my imperturbable zeal, with 5 stoves to heat up with damp wood and to maintain. There were to be no speeches in the Programme, in consequence of which the evening with our English guests from Bremke was very enjoyable - unaffected and carefree. English and German songs alternated in community singing. Günter played the concertina. We had great fun with comic songs like the one about the cross-eyed cook which David sang to us. As our guests who were now, sadly, quitting Bremke, took their leave we had a hilarious snowball battle. Have we not in the last years lost a lot of unconstrained and joyous community feeling?

Friday 1.3.46 We got up at the usual time, and as several had difficulty in detaching themselves from bed there was the usual chase about the ablutions to get to breakfast on time.

From 8 o'clock we continued our work on the three huts we began yesterday. Here we have had slow practice in this new activity and in separate work-groups, almost like jigsaws fitting together, the work went on quickly. By midday the whole inner skin was complete and about 3 pm the hut stood whole! We started the foundation and framing for the next hut and confirmed that our day's work produced one complete hut. Ramsay and Joachim got ready for the Sunday evening dance and called up the students for next week's IVSP unit.

The table tennis and chess tournaments had to be postponed as the discussion evening went on too long. Several topics were long, democratically and persistently debated, in part without any desire to inform. Some were against inviting more men to the dance evening. Did they not feel vigorous enough? To conclude the evening Ramsay gave us a further glimpse of the aims, work, ideas and organisation of IVSP. The discussion which so stimulated our minds that we lay sleepless for a long time, found its expression more in sound and fury than meaningful argument.

Saturday 2.3.46 After the long evening of discussion, which continued in the dormitory, rising was very difficult. It was good that we had a half day's work in front of us. After a magnificent breakfast of porridge, bread, butter and cheese we went to work, this time with spades, shovels and picks to dig roadside drains against the coming thaw. Many thought this not so good a job as hut building because progress and result can't be so accurately measured. Completed huts are more convincing. Every day work is interrupted by a hot cup of tea. At midday we had pancakes, potatoes and gravy that all went down well. We are being properly spoiled here - the smaller portions at home will be harder to bear. Most of us slept in the afternoon, some read or played as well as helping the 'Sisters' in the kitchen.

For dinner Marian and Anneliese had surpassed themselves: soup, roast beef with sauerkraut, suet pudding with fruit sauce (3 helpings!). An agreeable evening finished with table-tennis, chess, music and conversation. At intervals the Sisters provided little refreshments. GK

Sunday 3.3.46 Breakfast between 9 & 10, that was the only signal for getting up on this day. And look - either because one was used to the early rising or the Sunday breakfast lured, there everybody was punctually out of bed. The rest of the morning was essentially taken up with preparation for the evening's festivity. After rising from lunch at 2 o'clock, we had a drive to Bremke along with a walk to the Gleichen, two hills which had in former times been named [the matching pair] by our [Student] Confederacy*. After returning, a plentiful evening meal and departure to Gross Schneen, the scene of whatever was going to happen: a laden table awaited us which in the whole course of the evening was not cleared, and a matching bevy of dance-mad sisters in 'Fairy-clothes' (Addi enlightened us about these). In spite of rustic, folksy village music everybody soon got going - see Joachim, who caused so much turmoil that he finished up with his partner measuring his length on the parquet. Specially noteworthy was the gaiety of our English friends, reinforced by comrades from Bremke who taught us something of Scottish dances. At 10 o'clock the party came to an end: the Sisters were seen home and we had a lovely walk back to Friedland. The day drew to an end with talk gathered round our stove.

*But see, eg Aus der geschichte von Bremke, etc. (Leopold Ziemann, 1978) which shows Bremke linked with the name Gleichen from at latest the 13th century.

Monday 4.3.46 It is the last day of work in Friedland for our IVSP group. But as from the first talk to our group an attitude to the purpose of the work developed, there was no mood of leave-taking or breaking-up lassitude as might have been expected. With regard to the work it was determined not to leave anything unfinished, to complete huts that were started and to finish off the drainage so that we could have nothing to be ashamed of. So the work went quickly forward - Fred is as always one of the most indefatigable, and punctually at 5 o'clock in spite of the *atrocious weather the objective was attained. At the communal dinner Marian achieved the climax of her cooking skill in a richly abundant farewell meal.*

In the evening we sat together for the last time at our stove-fireside, jawing, singing, playing chess and watching Ramsay coming out victorious from a table-tennis tournament.

In the conversations of these days the wish emerged again and again to take up as a stimulus our short activity, to keep contact with our English friends and if possible work together again soon. Their movement with its motto "Deeds Not Words" has become a good example and has given us many good precepts to take with us on the way.

Tuesday 5.3.46 This was the day for leave-taking for most of the first week's team and the arrival day for most of the newcomers (2 arrived a day later). A last breakfast united us at the table and farewell speeches were exchanged. Joachim II speaking for all thanked Marian and Anneliese, Ramsay and Fred for the trouble they had taken for us and ended with "three cheers for our British friends". In his reply Ramsay said that the community spirit and understanding between the people of our countries was easier than he had expected. After that Marian had prepared a good packed lunch for the departees in the truck which Fred would drive to Göttingen. Before that though the first of the new arrivals had come, mostly Divinity students with thunderous trombones and in the camp many must wonder at the extraordinary music which reverberated in greeting. But afterwards the bedplaces, rubber boots and raincoats were issued and we were called to work; and we could be seen during the morning at the roadside drainage. In the afternoon we were on the huts and in the evening we diverted ourselves with table-tennis, chess and stimulating talk.

Wednesday 6.3.46 A singular awakening! Our three hardy brass-blowers standing unobserved outside in spite of the icy cold had with stiff fingers started to execute "Lobe den Herrn". That was truly a pretty nice arousal to a new day's work, and if occasionally a note was slightly off, so were, by an unpremeditated rehearsal, both players and listeners the more pleased by the rendering. It was at the same time a colder and damper day, so that we were painfully conscious of working with sheet metal. I remember having let a corrugated sheet fall from a height because

I had no feeling in my fingers. Having regard to the weather, from 10 o'clock the work was changed and the road cleared of snow. At the same time, what was even more practicable, to ensure a good run off for thaw water from each street. In the afternoon it went well with hutbuilding, and the four hours never went so quickly. In the evening there was a little review at our stoveside, in English and German, of simple and profound problems. Ramsay, Anneliese and Horst had an invitation to Bremke and went there immediately after dinner.

Thursday 7.3.46 *The day recorded a special note in our evening discussion - the day's work was in spite of the unkindness of the weather again completed. However, if we later on think back on this day we will above all remember the evening. It was arranged as a discussion on religious problems. Ramsay opened with a list of questions that addressed the actual direction of the present churches. In spite of the difficulty of the problems and the language hindrance the debate flowed on. There were the following trains of thought: The Church is not just 'a community of believers' but has an earthly aspect. This earthly aspect is of necessity concerned with earthly experiences. The common aim of Christians inside and outside the Church is the imitation of Christ, therefore preaching precedes action. It is a tragic consequence of imperfection when the achievements are so trifling. Christians outside the Church, Ramsay argued, consciously renounce mass influence and begin with action by themselves. The Church's way seems to them to be a diversion.*

Such a discussion seldom succeeds in reaching a conclusion. This one did. A happy judgment was reached: in spite of the difference of the routes, the end is the same.

Friday 8.3.46 *Again the day's course began with the reveille of our brass blowers and there followed then the actions as laid down in the day's master-plan: Washing, Breakfast, Work, Elevenses, Work, Lunch, Work and Dinner. We are already well accustomed to the way of living and grow closer daily to our English friends.*

In the evening we play some table-tennis and have general discussion about the work. We sing together a bit. We get special pleasure from 'Nine Green Bottles' and the English round 'Follow, follow' which we sing with great joy.

Saturday 9.3.46 *We spent a happy weekend without too much work. Because in the forenoon some of us helped the refugees with their luggage, our hut wasn't finished today as we had expected. The afternoon brought a visit from Anneliese's mother. The trombones practised for the choral evening when we have a party with the Sisters from the camp. After today's very plentiful dinner we all went to the big hall of the Friedland Inn; it gave an uncomfortable impression. However, as we sang one jolly song after another, enjoyed the most exciting English party games and Fred in little comic sketches caused great hilarity we found it very agreeable and were astonished how quickly the cheerful two hours had passed.*

In retrospect however one must say that the evening was a little extemporised, and the gratification of tongue and palate which Marian had provided and the enlivening cheerfulness of our Fred were to be thanked for its success.

Sunday 10.3.46 *Getting up on Sunday is not compulsory but voluntary. Coffee at 9. We have 'high tea' at 1 o'clock - very English. We have roast beef with raw white cabbage and Yorkshire pudding. That is pancake mix baked in plenty of fat in an oven.   Ramsay, our expert Yorkshireman, prepared it. For 'afters' we had apple pie, then coffee. After that the volunteers went with Fred Ramsay and Marian to Bremke, the English to bath (it's necessary!) and the volunteers to go for a walk. At half past 4 all returned and the two who stayed behind had prepared a complete high tea. Then to the theatre in Göttingen. Everybody enjoyed Mozart's 'Seraglio'. The journey there and back in an old noisy truck. With a good supper of cocoa and cakes the second Sunday with IVSP in Friedland ended.*

Monday 11.3.46 *Today the last hut was completed: this took up the morning. After a nourishing meal we went to lay the floor in the first hut; four men went with Fred to the old refugee camp and demolished a shelter roof there which would serve as weather protection for refugees waiting for their rations. Special events of this day:*

Heinz Papenfuss was 24 today and in the afternoon went to Göttingen to celebrate his birthday with his relatives, but to make up for him three new comrades arrived: Martin Storch (as 4th trombonist), Engelbert Kulenkampff — Rolf's brother — and Dieter Holtermann, Anneliese's and Horst's brother. The evening was taken up with a table-tennis tournament which developed into a merry game and at 11 o'clock there was another nourishing snack and community singing under Fred's direction.

Tuesday 12.3.46   *Punctuality at breakfast was to seek, because the kitchen-service had only half-heartedly awoken so that only some of them got up. After that a smaller group left as before for home, of whom some went back to Göttingen.   The newcomers arrived in dribs and drabs. Some built a garage for the Red Cross Ambulance, some laid further floors and a third group dug a trench to speed up clearance of the luggage. So went the day and afterwards as always we tried a first-rate supper to stretch our wits to get together an intelligent programme for Monday evening.   As several of us were shattered, we soon went to bed.*

Wednesday 13.3.46   *We won't forget this Wednesday in a hurry.   It began well and ended with a record achievement.   The breakfast was so good and plentiful that everyone was more than satisfied and the work went easily and smoothly.   One group did further work on the Red Cross garage, the other attended further to the drainage of the access road.   For supper we had a fantastic bean soup which gave us the strength to overcome the aftermath of work.   About 3000 expellees arrived and were deposited with their luggage on the road in front of the camp.   The people from the Home Mission with their handcarts couldn't cope.   We leapt in.   Ramsay drove his small truck continually back and forth.   With almost unbelievable speed unloading and loading went on.   Towards 11 o'clock the last families with their luggage were safe and we sank dead tired to sleep.   We were deeply satisfied in the consciousness that this day we had fully and completely done our duty.*

Thursday 14.3.46   *A specially important day in the life of IVSP.   In the morning a quick glance showed there was nothing to be seen of the half-finished hut.   Ramsay gasped in so much air birds were drawn in. So we had fresh work; instead of what was planned the hut was reborn. The other group had it easier; a once-laid floor cannot so quickly fall down.   It was well done, which because of our good feeding was no wonder! The evening passed with tennis, conversation and rehearsal for the 'Variety Concert', notably Otto's tremendous memory test (how long have you been in prison?). From 11.30 regular breathing and frequent forced marches in the night could be heard.   (Quite by the way, be it remarked the IVSP had this day the best kitchen-service.   Everybody knows it. No soliciting, please!)*

Friday 15.3.46
Essen - prima
Arbeit - gut aber nichts geneuch
Haus conference - viel sprechen ... the rest must be in English. We were rudely awakened by Arnold's trumpet performance, put on for Martin's special benefit. Work consisted of finishing the Nissen for the ambulance, continuing the flooring of the hospital block, and starting its fencing off. Shortage of materials has brought all these to a stop - Ramsay is in conference with the camp powers about our future job. Their ideas on urgency and priority work differ materially from ours.

Refugee traffic continues greater and transport for incomers small - some helped in baggage carrying. At the evening meeting "work" took a prominent place - Ramsay and Paul contributed; Fred outlined the social programme for the weekend, and the concert was discussed; Anneliese had some kitchen points; Ramsay drew attention to pilfering that had taken place in our store, and urged care on all. And then a little singing rehearsal before bed.

Sunday 17.3.46   This morning we found ourselves sitting together in only a quite small group - the Trombone Angels (Horst, Paul and Martin) had taken off to blast the ears of the farmers in several villages round about.

The day honoured its name: the sun shone again for the first time after so long a period and made everything bright and joyful. It was of course naturally so - when Angels travel, Heaven rejoices. In the afternoon we walked with Fred to the Holtermanns at Bremke. In continual conflict between one's own sense and Fred's declared routes we wandered through the beautiful sun-streaked wood until luckily we arrived one and a half hours late in Bremke. Ramsay sits there, as long as he can, at the piano and played Brahms, Schubert etc. It was hard for him, that he had to leave early. After the evening meal - 'high tea' today - we all together again talked about "I.V.S.P", what IVSP was doing in Belgium, Holland, Norway and in Germany since the invasion and about the future tasks and goals. We dream of a reunion in Münster, since Fred and Ramsay are going there to help in 3 camps for evacuees and refugees and restore them to their dwellings.

Monday 18.3.46 *An exciting day! The Variety Concert and changeover of work parties determine its complexion. Then unexpectedly in the morning the troop of new students arrived, who were not due until Tuesday. But IVSP coped with them: Ramsay and Fred certainly deserved special praise and above all Marian! Besides the continuing work, in the afternoon we had a visitation from a General but with all this IVSP's extensively advertised Variety evening for the Friedland camp staff was not purely an improvisation. It was in fact a consummate success: Music, Magic, Songs and Sketches. Thanks to all those who worked behind the scenes, who sat down with us for a short hour! Above all, thanks to IVSP: the manner of the organisation of the evening in its freedom, happiness and its reconciliatory freshness must have made an impression on all who saw it. For us however it meant the conclusion of a week's work and the spirit that out of this preparation will for us students have its effect in future: the voluntary fulfilment of the advancement of higher human mission, to give reciprocal help, to labour with one another and to maintain the struggle against distress and destruction.*

Tuesday 19.3.46 *As we sat at breakfast Jürgen came and then during the morning, Hubert and Gerhard. For the morning Ramsay divided us into two groups, one to help load the refugees while we completed the digging of the drain on the road to Camp B by 12. In the afternoon the first group went on with their work and we searched for the drainpipe of the road to the loading ramp, as it had been damaged, and found it after much trouble. In the evening Ramsay spoke about the foundation, work and range of activities of IVSP.*

Wednesday 20.3.46 *Today also we worked in several groups in bright weather. We started with the demolition of a washing hut, to be rebuilt on the mound in camp B. Ramsay wanted to make a bet with the sceptical deputy camp chief that the hut would be set up ready on Monday, but he scratched the back of his head and wouldn't take it, knowing our rate of working. Otherwise the refugees were helped with loading and in the newly created hut part of the floorboarding had to be laid. At long last the repair to the drain proved itself, but not finally, because the camp administration, as soon as the new pipe was laid, came with an order to cement the joints. Therefore this job will be finished tomorrow. In the evening everyone pleased himself, plans for the dance on Sunday* were forged and Martin made us laugh with tales of his time as a sailor ... Corrugated iron is already bent, and fortunately rafters have nothing to do with us...

Thursday 21.3.46 *Strengthened by a good breakfast we threw ourselves into work. Three units again worked, one on the drains, one on the floors and the other which in this case was the majority, on the demolition of the washing hut and the shifting of the pieces. We worked so fast that the hut disappeared and there was no more work. After a very short forced interval we began to take another washing hut apart and got well on with it in the afternoon.*

The evening was to be taken up with discussion of a letter from a German friend of the Frenchman Albert Camus. Starting with the letter we discussed first the fundamental question, whether justice governs a particular people or whether any objective can be made subject to it. People acknowledged the idea of justice with the reservation that it is in the practical life of the individuals and peoples often very difficult to carry out. Then we came to the question of the future constitution of Europe. It was stressed that in contrast to former and present policies people must work much closer together without considering only their own advantage. Our English friends spoke of the responsibility of the individual for his government and also for other peoples. We are grateful to them that they acknowledged that with reference to our people they had not fully done their duty.

Friday 22.3.46 *On a good foundation we worked throughout the day again in several groups. The work on the drainage, on demolition of the second washing hut and on laying floors proceeded with heightened ardour as we come to the end of this work on Saturday. An extra gang made itself useful in putting up fences.*

The evening passed in a great variety of ways, first a report by Ramsay on the activities gave an appreciation of the work we accomplished, then Martin as master of ceremonies explained his programme for the dance on Saturday, David gave an insight into the future work of IVSP from which arose a particular hope to get foreign volunteers as well to their work in the future and so bring nearer the achievement of common purpose. There was also mention of the participation of German volunteers in services abroad. A guest from

Berlin who had passed the evening with us and had accordingly got to know our special openness and comradeship provoked displeasure and great aversion when he being questioned about the situation in Berlin, waffling around the subject only yielded cautious 'Press-releases'. One could from these answers conclude that this gentleman seems not to have come out from his four walls in the American Zone; which left us with the unhappy impression that this man was quite unsuitable for creating a working community in the IVSP sense. Community singing led by Fred however lifted the nightmare and let the evening die away in the usual harmonious manner.

The Last Day - Saturday 23.3.46

1   *The corrugated iron shed*
        Unheated in dawn's gleams
        Invites no leap from our straw-bed
        In spite of troubled dreams.

2   *We indolently lie and tussle*
        With our impediment
        When we should raise some moral muscle
        From solid fundament.

3   *This is no average demand*
        That regiments us here
        Conscience has called us: here we stand
        Each one a VOLUNTEER.

4   *Pity the man whose conscience stretches*
        As far as it will run,
        And hurries to pull on his britches
        When breakfast's nearly done.

5   *Following breakfast, work's allotted;*
        A drag, then young and bright
        With IVSP zeal besotted
        We set out to the site.

6   *But ... yesterday ... a hut stood there ...*
        We built it, and we knew.
        Our eyes' report, drawn from their stare
        In no way could be true.

7   The wind that blew throughout the night
    Contrived a thorough blitz.
    It blew a storm with all its might
    And there's the hut in bits.

8   The Boreal blast's skill, old and good,
    At our spilled sweat had jeered -
    Not for the last time David stood
    Astonished in his beard.

9   We spat then on our freezing mitts
    And gladly got them working,
    Dismantling eagerly the bits
    Among the wreckage lurking.

10 Our many jobs insight affording
    Those watching us can sense:
    While one is laying down duckboarding
    Another mends the fence.

11 A General with no known name
    Invites himself today;
    To Ramsay it is all the same
    If he's not asked to play.

12 The weather thinks that April's here
    And rain's the season's norm:
    We're clad in hoods and duffle gear
    Like gnomes against the storm.

13 And during work there's always questing -
    Opinions right and left,
    Fluent and fluid, interesting,
    East-West the warp and weft.

14 Among such diff'rent intuitions
    Often the way's not seen,
    But unity, with Luck's additions
    Can find the golden mean.

15 The midday meal at twelve is due
    (The time is checked by Fred).
    Like omnivores at any zoo
    The ravening horde is fed.

16 He feels as if - does every man -
    He's in a Paradise,
    And lauds the skill of Marian,
    The worth of Annelies'.

17 Today is Saturday, and so
    The afternoon to fill,
    Each one is free at once to go
    And do whate'er he will.

18 With Anneliese Ramsay's set
    Spazieren gehn, zum Spass:
    But a piano he must get
    For party time, alas.

19 With fevered haste and eager face
    The place he sought he found.
    He drove the truck at breakneck pace
    Bouncing along the ground.

20 But others sought themselves to grace
    In idle soapy suds.
    (As in the Book our lives we trace
    We're under Preachers' Kids!).

21 We pass the time in merry guise
    With tales to prod our feeling,
    And that is great.   It brings a prize
    Like doing the spud-peeling.

22 Gunther enthralled us with a tale
    Of twinlets so ideal
    They must renounce this tearful vale
    For only death is real.

23 For such a day, with swelling hearts,
    At six we sat at table
    And ate spuds, ham and eggs and tarts -
    As much as we were able.

24 Then we got ready for the party
    We'd planned with much hubris.
    The wifely guests greeted their hearty
    Husbands with a kiss.

25   Hubert had travelled while dark fell
      To make one at the ploy.
      His family he'd left quite well -
      All uncles, to a boy.

26   Not a few came to join the train,
      In Sunday best rigged out;
      But as they danced with might and main
      They cast the surplus clout.

27   Lord! Who can contemplate such fall!
      Cut down's the urban swagger.
      They dance in Gross Schneen Gasthof's hall
      Like any rustic beggar.

28   The Polonaise on spring-heels sped
      (With luck thro' cross-aisle slipping)
      And unforgettable was Fred
      In Highland leaps and skipping.

29   Our team produced a bunch of cronies
      Attuned to Music's spell
      Who notwithstanding creaking bonies
      Stepped high and wide and well.

30   We danced with vigour till at last
      This to our sense was clear -
      More folk were coming thick and fast:
      The whole village was here,

31   Till finally, where music rang,
      Where there was tea and cakes,
      Where we still jollier ditties sang:
      That was just what it takes.

32   With sketch and song and what you will
      The ending came too soon.
      Ramsay with serio-comic skill
      Reviewed what we had done.

33   Outside the stars shone clear and bright
      Beneath the heaven's dome.
      With cheerful thanks we said goodnight
      And saw the ladies home.

34   *We sat ourselves down all together*
I' the corrugated shed
And poked the stove and had a blether,
Cocoa and buttered bread.

35   *And while we lazed in slippered ease,*
The camp in quietude,
Friend Martin spoke frivolities
And kittledaddledu'd.

36   *And thoroughly he played the priest*
Attentively heard by all,
Till all the talk slowed down and ceased:
Two thirty's on the dial.

37   *Then under DDTed cover*
We sought and found repose,
Some sense in dreamland to discover
Before our eyes unclose.

38   *That land of dreams now out of reach -*
Where think you can it be?
Instead of arms - does it so teach -
Is it - IVSP?

Jürgen [Hess]

[The attentive reader will have noted that Jürgen, who arrived on the 19th, celebrated the last day partly by plagiarising and embellishing his departed colleagues' reports, producing a poetic symposium of the whole service]

Sunday 24.3.46 *Sunday sun standing triumphant over Friedland camp awoke after an all-too-short night the sleepers laid out from rhythmic and intellectual acrobatics and enticed them away from a happy breakfast table to a walk through Reckershausen. In reflective conversation were spring flowers and old wisdoms newly discovered, airy badinage fluttered from mouth to mouth like butterflies, and yet - for whom was it not so - that through all the yearnings and hopes for the future ever and again the experiences of the past years of war burned? Today there stands in the centre the idea of practical voluntary work beyond the boundaries of separate nations in the service of peace. Why should we not acknowledge that it was not easy for us to come to this conclusion? The energetic* *example of our British friends, the discussions in small groups and between individuals brought us close to this purpose so that this voluntary time of work in spite of its brevity granted us more than mere understanding. Thoughts follow action: as we reached Friedland camp again we could lay hold of the as yet unbroken refugee-chain. And the Sunday meal tasted specially good in the "joyful consciousness of duty done."*

The afternoon passed in dolce far niente and after a good meal we hastened to Göttingen where in the theatre Verdi's Otello should have inspired us. Was it the stark contrast after a week of unaccustomed hard labour .. was it a few superficialities in the performance .. or the spoiled city folk overlooking the honourable endeavours of the cast to let such different meanings come out .. ? The really good orchestral performance must however have more than compensated any lover of Verdi's music.

As we all united late in the evening round the central glowing stove a bitter little drop fell into our steaming cocoa - the realisation of the last day of the German-British community, and this was: NOT good enough for IVSP.

Letter, 2/3/46, FJM to Alastair.

IVSP FRIEDLAND

On Thursday on terrible roads of snow, ice & slush I came via Goslar while Dave went straight home on the 'new' Mercedes which we 'won' at HQ5. We turned up at the social evening at the Scheme and found everything going swell — and little wonder as they are a good bunch of lads and as we sat round a stove and sang English-German song about, I thought how well they fitted into an IVSP company. They were all about 20-30 most of them having served in the Army (& one was a Major) and if they can be taken as representing German youth it certainly is not true to say they lack humour as even in English they make many real good cracks. Dave & I left early along with Betty & Arthur Brown - the former as we still had to pack and the latter as they were going to Berlin — and the parting was made with quite a depth of feeling especially by Horst & Anneliese who we knew in the village. And this was repeated next morning by the Jüttes and I am committed to return to Bremke at some time or other - a pleasure I look forward to.

Letter, 2/3/46, FJM to Alastair.

AS OTHERS SEE US

On Tuesday Dave & I went to Vlotho - Dave to attend a conference and I in the hope of picking up a lorry. We met many kent faces but by a bit of strategy managed to get to bed reasonably early. Next morning I went in search of spares at the request of the Transport Officer as I was free and went to Herford to pick up a new vehicle. I got back in time to be given a Signal that all was in order for us to move. In the evening we tried to write some letters but were not too successful as people came along and indulged in chaff. We finally decided to get to bed early and Dave made off but I fell for the temptation of a cup of coffee offered by one of the Red Cross Typists on whom IVSP members usually sharpened their wits as she is a cheeky bit of goods. She was in provocative mood and had a few pointed remarks about IVSP's attitude to German Welfare stating that she couldn't understand why she liked the IVSP when they were so minded and further added that she was glad Red Cross were pulling out before they became too much involved. This started it as I pointed out that we were not concerned so much with German welfare as human welfare and regarded a man or woman as primarily human with nationality of secondary consideration and by thus approaching each as an individual we were prepared to consider each on his merits - thus we were more prepared to admire the qualities of a good German before the qualities of a bad Englishman, & so on & so on with all the issues of pacifism etc arising. In the end - by the time the coffee was finished at approx 12.15 - she came away with the remark that she thought conchies were all bloody fools (some likeable none the less) but they were so damned logical that she was going to stop arguing with them.

NEW JOB - NEW SURROUNDINGS

We ultimately got packed and into bed to waken and find that it had snowed overnight which made our 200 km run even more formidable. As Dave had been even later in getting to bed than I had I drove first and it was as tricky a job as I've had for long enough as even a careless gear change was enough to skid the car on the rink-like surface and once it started to skid it was about 300 yds before you were sure that you would stay in the way you wished to go. After crossing the Weser we had to put on snow chains to enable us to mount a four-bend hill climb but avoided the yawning ditches on either side which had welcomed several others. In one piece we reached Warendorf and were told the location of our new billets but on getting there found the Burgermeister did not have the key and by way of completing the picture we had barely turned when the front spring of the car broke, but we had fortune in misfortune and a nearby REME towed us in and put the car under guard for the night while we slept in the Guard Room.

We are to be responsible for the absorbing into the population of the expellees from New Poland but no one is exactly aware of what is going to be what.

The teams in Europe have been asked to supply two volunteers to join an FAU group going to Norway and I have been playing with the idea but from selfish motives I hold back. If Dave cannot raise other names I may yet find myself working for IVSP in civvies and it wouldn't be a bad thing as this pseudo Officer business is breaking my morale and I now come to regard physical comfort as part of my dues.

"OPERATION SWALLOW"

HWR

From now on, the work of Unit 4 arose directly from the Potsdam Agreement (in truth a disagreement) between the Allies regarding the post-war frontier of Germany. The frontiers of Poland, East and West, were moved westwards. Between February and September 1946 8 million Germans were to be deported from the new territory of Poland and resettled and absorbed into Germany reduced in size and in the stagnation of defeat. Military

Government called this "Operation Swallow". Expellees arrived by the trainload, were directed to transit camps, then dispersed. Initially Unit 4 supervised one arrival railhead at Rheine in Westphalia.

Letter, 10/3/46, FJM to his family:

NEW BILLETS

When I left you last week-end I was writing you in the Officers Mess at Warendorf but on Monday morning we decided we would leave such luxury and go and try and put our house in order. In the afternoon Dave came to the billet which up to a fortnight ago had been an Officers Mess but was now rather barren of furniture as the retiring Unit had made sure their next nest would be furnished. Having left Dave I went to Melle, about 62 km away with the broken spring and managed to get the job of repair put in hand. Just as I entered the bad stretch of road I made up on a lorry and was surprised to see the Guides sign on the back and even more surprised when on looking back I saw Albert Harris and Dorothy aboard. We arrived in to find Dave trying to cook a dinner in a couple of mess tins and boil water in a - Jerry. Did we laugh? - and when at that particular moment it split with a pop we simply howled.

CHANGE IN THE AIR

On Thursday Dave and I accompanied the Major under whom we are supposed to operate and he is a real Col Blimp - "Let the blighters do the job themselves - they'll do it if they are kicked into action and I am the one to do it, etc." He is completely new to the job and when we got to Rheine and saw the accommodation Dave and I thought it was a palace by comparison with most transit camps we have seen and yet he was shocked and kept spluttering about them being human beings and not cattle. The accommodation was formerly barracks and the floors in each room were very clean and a straw palliasse was filled and ready for each person. He thought they should have some sort of bed until we pointed out how seriously that was going to cut down accommodation and the material used could no doubt be more profitably used elsewhere.

Yesterday I got a letter asking me to take on the leadership of this Unit. This caused me a bit of a headache as I am not at all satisfied that we are justified in staying out here as a 'Relief' team much longer and as a result of this have written to London for more details of the scheme in Norway. It may be that I am wrong and that some real relief work remains to be done but I feel that if given the material and something to work for 'Gerry' is now quite able to look after himself. I don't think it is an IVSP job to go around picking holes in what someone else does just to justify us swanking around in cars and living as parasites. Don't get me wrong - there is still plenty 'misery' but the German organisations are not helpless when it comes to helping their own people. There are other lines in which IVSP might develop but as it is the Leadership of a Relief Section they ask me to take on I do not feel it wise to accept and have written John accordingly. Let us hope the McLaren stock does not fall too low!

1 ENGLISH BLONDE = ? SCOTS

Don't ask me why but we Scots seem to be much more in love with our homeland than any of the English members of the Unit - and out here it is an excellent trade-union and means of introduction. I would say that next to Mary it is the surest way of getting something that otherwise we have difficulty in obtaining. Mary, Frau Jessett as Ian calls her, can work wonders on the poor QMs in the army and when she went for rations yesterday she mentioned that we were short of certain items and returned laden down with as much as she wanted of everything. We have stipulated that the replacements must include an attractive blonde - preferably without husband this time - but are not too hopeful.

Letter, 18/3/46, FJM to his family:

CONTACTS AT ALL POINTS

This will be my last letter written in Germany as I leave for England this evening to prepare for departure to Norway. This is the outcome of my turning down the leadership of this Unit - when they heard I was not tied up in that capacity they wired me to ask if I would return immediately to attend a course at the FAU training centre at Birmingham which begins on the 20th.

I only got word on Friday at lunch time and since then I have been back at Bremke - I could not leave this country without saying goodbye to the friends we made there and also to Fred, Ramsay and Marian who are still on the Work-scheme. I left on the Adler and in glorious weather made good time and for most of the way had the company of three soldiers who like me were returning to visit old haunts. They only expected to get taken to the station at Holzminden where they hoped to get a train to Northeim - you can imagine their reaction when they heard that I could take them the whole distance. They gave me an interesting sidelight into the effect different troops can have on the population as the lot that came in to relieve them are having continual trouble in a village where previously everything was harmonious. They blame the new Comm. Officer who has imposed all sorts of restrictions and has even prohibited the return of visitors from the former company - the lads have to cut through woods and get into a farm house and on the signal going round the village the people come along with their letters for other members of the former Battalion.

I got to Friedland to find the students rehearsing for a concert and Fred had made quite a good effort at putting over the gags we did at Hermitage parties. They seem just as funny when done in German. The scheme has been a huge success. Dave at the moment is trying to 'sell' the idea to the Control Commission and it may be possible that some may be on Harvest schemes. In the evening I went up to Bremke and at the Jüttes especially the departure was most touching. Fritz who spent almost all his army service in Norway has given me a list of addresses he wishes me to try and contact as he had a very pleasant time while over there. It seems strange that friendship should have been shown to the invaders if they were as they were painted. Fritz admits that he was ashamed of the behaviour of some of his comrades but does not think they were worse than any occupying force would be. That incidentally is his opinion and I am not drawing any conclusions as experience in Holland prevents me jumping to a decision.

I got back here at 12.30 to find that the Guides had come up from Dortmund to be in on my farewell dinner - it is amazing how news travels up here as my departure had been casually mentioned to their liaison officer by Dave and she had been to see them and passed on the news.

Taped Recollections, Stan Slee

QUIS CUSTODIET IPSOS CUSTODES ?

Our team was to act as what I like to think of as a guardian *ad litem* when an adoption is being arranged. He has nothing to do with the actual adoption, but has to make sure no one is under any misapprehension about what's happening. They must all be aware of the permanence of what is happening, and everything that has to be done must be observed and made to happen.

Inter-Allied agreements said that the respective Zone armies were responsible for the movement of expellees across their zones, but the local German authorities were responsible for feeding them en route and for regular medical checks particularly to spot parasites that could spread disease. The latter were also responsible for ensuring that they were integrated within a community of reception and not just dumped in camps.

We and similar teams had to make sure all this happened. For instance I rode on trains from Friedland right across Germany to the Dutch frontier area, making sure there were adequate meals available at the approved times. When later we were transferred to working at the other end of the re-settlement transports, I

Being sprayed with DDT to combat lice

remember we were constantly warned of the danger of typhus, and of the need to enforce the medical examination regulations.

As we were expecting a train-load of expellees I went down to the station and was surprised to find that there was transport waiting outside the station - lorries and buses - and no sign of the local German authorities. I made enquiries and there was an army officer there from the Town Major's office. "Oh, no, he said, there's been a change here. The Town Major has arranged for the people to be bussed straight to the villages where they're going to be settled, because he doesn't want to run the risk of typhoid spreading through the town." This meant they would not have had any medical examination.

I had no authority to overrule his decision but I did know many of the bus drivers and some of the local officials. One of them had turned up and was shrugging his shoulders and saying it wasn't their idea; this was what the military had arranged. I was able to persuade him to get a church hall opened, and I told all the bus drivers to go back home and come back in the morning. I rang back to our unit to bring up our stock of emergency food - knäckebrot from Scandinavia, butter, jam, milk and cocoa powder and sugar. I also rang our Red Cross HQ in Vlotho and told them what I was doing. The Assistant Commissioner, Admiral Bevan, agreed that medical examination was essential under the circumstances and was prepared to take the matter to Army HQ.

Meanwhile the Town Major himself turned up raging about his orders being countermanded. All I could do was to say we couldn't countermand them again, but that I would see him about the whole thing next morning.

Next morning he had been called to his HQ. I did not see him again.

AND COME WHAT MAY, I HAVE BEEN BLESSED (BYRON)

Eileen Taylor (Unit 7)

As the Bishop of Xanten passed he refused us his blessing. His hand fell to his side; his mitred head turned away. I was shocked.

It was in March 1946 — Kevelaer, a once handsome village 20 km West from the Rhine. Our IVSP team, 6 men, 6 women, occupied the only house that had retained a roof. The Church, abnormally large for a village, was an empty shell but it was still visible across the wide plain of the Nieder Rhein, and its spire, a crooked chimney of reddish stone, still pointed an arthritic finger heavenwards.

The Bishop was escorting home to Kevelaer its greatest possession, the Weeping Madonna. She had been buried during the war for safety deep within the vaults of Xanten Cathedral. The grey procession of half-starved people shuffled past our billet and their muttered chanting hung like a swarm of gnats in the freezing air. The slow crunch, crunch, crunch of their feet splintering the ice-laced puddles along the pitted road was as melancholy a sound as I had ever heard. They had walked 10 kilometres that bitter morning. The Bishop was weak with hunger and fatigue.

Behind him came the cart on which she had been erected beneath a tinselled canopy. Four men pulled her along, four men so bowed with strain, so dull in colour that for a fleeting moment I thought they were donkeys, but only for a moment for in that devastated countryside no animal remained alive. The Madonna, a glittering doll-like effigy with painted cheeks, seemed oblivious of her surroundings. She swayed somewhat tipsily as the cart lurched in the ruts, but indifferent to her one could not be, for the towering golden crown on her head and the stiff fan-spread dress encrusted with jewels cast an aureole of light. She was unearthly, a vision from whose protruding eyes tears had been seen to fall, staining, like dirty brush strokes, the too pink patina of the cheeks. She was famous throughout the Rhineland and for centuries pilgrims had travelled, penitentially barefooted, the long straight roads to her shrine. From time to time she wept for them. Without her the inhabitants of Kevelaer felt lost and within the shell of the nave they had built her with bare hands a new shrine from the stones of the old. Even before they attempted to rebuild their own homes. We were not wanted.

Our team were abnormally quiet during the next few days. CharlieB and I still went off each morning on our scheduled tour of the ruined villages seeking out doctors, for we had a consignment of medical supplies to distribute. It was a heart-breaking task and we were shaken with compassion. I had never seen a dead body or a child's head crawling with maggots. The doctors broke down and wept, their tears falling far more copiously than those of their Madonna. I could not get her out of my mind.

CharlieB was my co-driver and work-mate. He was a tubby easy-going fellow hiding a thoughtful and sensitive disposition behind a somewhat lascivious manner. 'Come into me arms, me booful' he would sing out to every *fräulein* we passed and he pouted his lips blowing suggestive noises ... yum-yum. He played this game as one tilting a lance at the Army orders posted up amid the rubble of the Town Hall: "No Fraternization", now out of date. I was fond of Charlie B. We had a comfortable working relationship. Only I knew that he had just become engaged back home. His invitations to the *fräuleins* never went further than yum-yum. It was his gesture of reconciliation.

It was a month later that we took the road, straight as a ruler, to Xanten. The team had decided we should explain to the Bishop who we were - men and women dedicated to the relief of distress. We would explain that we were allowed to help in this way only on condition that we wore British khaki uniform, which understandably must have presented an unwelcome picture to him. CharlieB and I had volunteered to try to do this. Trees fringing either side drew the converging lines of perspective, taut and graceful, to a distant point on the horizon. Spring green tipped the bronze buds and the sky gleamed, benign with faint warmth.

On the crest of a gentle hill, the only rising ground on that flat plain, our truck stopped. No tinkering with the engine would make it budge. It could not be left there: vehicles were apt to disappear if left unattended. We had already lost two. Leaving CharlieB on guard I marched back down the hill to the battered village we had just passed through. Between broken slabs of concrete a makeshift door bore one word. Bürgermeister. I pushed it. In the dim light I must have appeared as an apparition for there was a scuffle as the Bürgermeister backed up against the wall and flung up his hands. It took quite a while to sort out that situation for my German was poor and he had no knowledge of English.

The miracle was that he had a single telephone line, a home-made wire loop across the country to the Police in Xanten. Voices could be heard disjointed and faint, but contact we had. After a long time, and while we were sipping "mucki-fucki" - a disgusting coffee made from the debris of the hedge-rows - a call crackled over the wire. The British Red Cross HQ in Vlotho, 300 km away had tried in vain to contact Kevelaer. They would try again later. That was all that could be done. Horrified to find that two hours had passed, the afternoon over, I stumbled off scattering a largesse of 'Danke-schön's until out of earshot.

Half-way up the hill I stopped dead. The truck was gone. Where was CharlieB? Had he been murdered and the vehicle stolen? Such things did happen. The little copse by the road revealed nothing. No sign of struggle, no blood. It was unthinkable that CharlieB would have abandoned me. Suddenly I realised how silent it all was, save for my thumping heart, unbelievably silent, not even the tiniest click of insect ... nothing. I stood limp in the road unable to move and confused by indecision. I was alone in the world. The shock of abandonment was terrifying.

How long it was before the sound came, I do not know. It was dark, moonless and starless. But there it was, a sweet bubbling trill. I was so numbed with misery that my mind scarcely acknowledged the possibility of sound. It came again, nearer, a bubbling rich trill followed by a soft tiu-tiu that rose ecstatically into a crescendo of brilliant notes. Nightingale. Somewhere in the invisible trees it was singing. Presently others joined in, flinging their exquisite crescendos about me, vibrating the night air with the power and glory of their song. From utter misery I soared to joy, spellbound. No matter what happened nothing could take their gift from me. I was blessed. And as the chorus began so it ended gradually until one last sweet trill ... one more ... one more and then no more.

And far away in the darkness two pin-points of light, headlights. They were coming for me. I knew it was them. I opened my arms and waited. They were calling and shouting. Up the hill they roared bathing me in light. The whole team was there, CharlieB at the wheel. They lifted me on to the truck, wrapped me in blankets. I could hear the relief in their voices, and I fell, at peace, into a deep sleep dimly conscious of their voices singing *Dona nobis pacem* as they took me home to Kevelaer.

Later I asked CharlieB what had happened. The truck had suddenly decided to start up. He had driven straight back to Kevelaer, not daring to stop. 'You knew I would come for you', he said. Did I? I did not mention the nightingales.

We never saw the Bishop. Within a few days we were transferred to Duisburg and civilian blue replaced our khaki. The Bishop's blessing no longer mattered to me. I had been blessed.

SNAPSHOT - KEVELAER

HWR (Unit 7)

During spare-time cricket practice on the sportsfield, a ball was struck hard to the boundary. A curious and well-meaning German stopped it with his foot. He regretted it ...

SNAPSHOTS - DUISBURG

Norman Lancashire(Unit 7)

In Duisburg I once with other team members was shown round a bombed hospital by a German sister or matron. Without rancour, she told us that we were in the ruins of what had been the children's ward. There were pathetic little beds, blackened and twisted. Had the children been got out? No, they had all been burned alive.

Scraps from the Rich Man's Table

I had a regular job, driving a vehicle to the barracks in Duisburg, where from the mess of the Highland Regiment squaddies I would collect a steel drum (presumably clean inside) full of the pieces of half-eaten bread and butter I found on the tables after meals. There were three orphanages administered by nuns to which I delivered the drums on a three-day rota. What I found most shame-making was the genuine gratitude and pleasure shown by the nuns on my arrival. They used to lay a big white sheet on the floor, and have these scraps tipped on to it.

Our Unit also had Army rations, which used to feed us well, in addition to a German catering couple, secretary, cook, maid and one or two cleaners. And our dustbins were regularly relieved of potato peelings.

EXTRACTS FROM A DIARY

Harry Robertson (Unit 7)

DUISBURG 1946-47

Duisburg had been the "largest inland port in Europe", and had had a famous opera company and house. In 1946 the port was derelict, the opera gone and the house seriously damaged. The people looked worse than any I saw in the whole of West Germany. They wandered about, stood in tram queues, shabby, pale, slow-moving, in a city which they could scarcely hope ever to see restored. Yet in ten minutes one can be out of the city centre and in charming country - woods of beech and deep gorge-like valleys. But fresh air breeds appetite.

BERLIN AUGUST 1946

The pretentious architecture of Berlin, apeing a style which, before the invention of the arch used columns with lintel over, was every-where to be seen. These columns are monstrous here even after so many have been destroyed. Those which remain often reveal their spurious nature when the plaster has fallen away, exposing the bricks beneath. Possibly the style pays tribute to a national character - Prussian perhaps. These patches where the plaster has fallen seemed significant.

We drove through the Russian sector, through the Brandenburger Tor, and later into the French sector. To visit the IVSP work-camp at Nikolassee we had to go into the American sector. The USSR army guards were very impressive-looking. People on the streets looked better fed than those in the west, but not so cheerful. In the S-bahn the crowd was cosmopolitan. A group of returning PoW from the east came by. They looked so "driven", so "gutted"; their eyes were the eyes of men utterly demoralised and subdued. In a shop in the Unter den Linden (Russian Sector) there was an impressive exhibition of the immediate past, present and hoped-for future of Berlin: the scheme for the new street plan, the figures for the repairs of dwellings, 50% of which had been destroyed, for the recovery of education - the intake of the universities, the census of teachers and the training of new ones. This was the most hopeful half hour I spent in Germany. I paid one Mark for a packet of pictures, and the man showed me a photograph of himself as he had been, and patted his jacket now so ample for his shrunken frame.

An old woman was grubbing out roots of a pavement tree, long since brought down. The Tiergarten no longer exists as a place where trees grow. Almost all have gone. There remains a company of destroyed statuary. Among the new things are the giant Bunker which it has taken the Allies so much and so long to destroy; and the allotments.

In the Russian sector I spoke with the gangs of women, clearing away rubble by chains of baskets, out of basements to the street above. They had been apprehended as collaborators. They were of all ages. I did not discover whether they received heavy workers' rations for this futile work. I visited several flats, often only partially habitable, all shabby, where large families were housed in few rooms. We were distributing clothes from the clothing store. We visited a settlement of bombed-out families. As elsewhere, the conditions varied with the will of the women to make do. Some of the huts let in rain and the sanitary conditions were unspeakably bad. If only this situation were an emergency of short duration.

We went to collect several old women from Spandau to move them to another home in the outskirts of the city. Before our journey was completed, one old woman had lost her dinner and we had to get the people at the destination to swill out the vehicle, for the vehicle was to take our rations back to the billet!

SCHLESWIG

A Summary of reports from team members
Basil Eastland (Senior Representative)

The very severe winter of 1946/7, in contrast with the comparatively mild one of 1945/6, heightened the misery of people, already under-nourished, visibly so in clothes too big for their bodies. Everything edible was rationed, even cabbages. Social security benefit was often insufficient to purchase the full rations. Few people could afford black market food, even if paid for in kind with their precious possessions. The team's own British rations could and did feed themselves and still provide three meals a day to three kitchen staff, plus two meals a day for three interpreters and visitors of all sorts.

The people had no money left over for fuel - wood , peat, brown coal, coal dust, used engine oil or saw-dust - and if there was electricity, the supply was frequently cut, to conserve national supplies; no money left over for clothes - a problem especially acute for returning prisoners of war, who could not begin to regain self-respect nor look for work without at least a respectable pair of trousers - nor for shoes, even if you could give the necessary proof that you had none, to qualify you for a coupon; mothers and teenage daughters frequently shared the same dress. This and the fact that there was no money left over for fares meant that people were marooned in their camp.

With the passing of the months and years, health standards fell. Hospitals were over-crowded and under-stocked. The very nurses developed TB as their resistance became lowered. The soap ration for every one and for all purposes was half a cake a month. There was a shortage of hair-brushes and combs, and toothbrushes: 80% of children had defective teeth. All refugees were automatically de-loused on arrival. The many children with scabies were treated with benzyl-benzoate. The team's first priority was always to inspect camp lavatories. Water supply was often inadequate. There were bed-bugs and fears of epidemics, very real in view of the incidence of TB and VD. Expectant mothers sought in vain for nappies, cot blankets and baby clothes.

All this took place in cramped accommodation, with three or four families (extended families at that) in one room - a room in such varied places as cellars beneath rubble, air raid shelters without windows, an ancient castle, hotels (awaiting lucrative custom and resenting refugees), a deserted lighthouse, a nunnery, leaky wooden huts of all sizes, huge draughty army barrack blocks, abandoned schools and other people's homes, where again they were less than welcome. They slept on loose straw, sea-grass, even seaweed, without covers, without bed-steads. They cooked as they could, using perhaps an old steel helmet to boil water. Until rebuilding began, using rubble-based materials, and until the few undamaged buildings began to be de-requisitoned from the occupying forces, these conditions could not but deteriorate. The prospect of such squalor becoming even worse was the final blow to those whose homes had formerly been models of hygiene and order.

Such conditions combined with hopelessness, apathy and boredom led to moral decay. Many families had already been broken up by death and physical loss, now in a country where the proportion of women to men was 13:9, the temptation to believe that the prisoner-of-war husband would never return led to other relationships, prostitution, neglect of children and consequent delinquency. There were bands of "wandering youths". There were the deserted wives and children of British soldiers. The black market played into the hands of greedy opportunists. The terrible material destruction caused by the war seemed less tragic compared with the physical, spiritual and moral deterioration of the men, women and children whom the team members encountered in the camps.

Education suffered: in one room, one teacher might have to cope with 50 children between the ages of 6 and 14, sharing text books and writing in the margins of old newspapers. A school built for 300 pupils would have 900, and work on a shift system - each child receiving about 2 hours' schooling per day.

An unreal political climate persisted: women, who under Hitler were inferior, had to learn the responsibilities and privileges of democratic government. The first local elections were held in September 1946. An unreal currency circulated, the real one being cigarettes, coffee or valuables, until the reform in June 1948, when a maximum of 40 new DM was allowed to each person. An unreal belief circulated, that a war against the much-hated Soviet Union was imminent and obvious. Polish people who remained in Germany, too afraid to return, were regarded with animosity. People were envious of the quite large Danish-speaking minority who received food parcels. A genuine grievance was that no one had explained why Germans had been evicted from Pomerania, Silesia and East Prussia. No one seemed to have heard of the Potsdam agreement. The majority did not know the truth about concentration camps, nor that gypsies had been among their victims. Few admitted to being active Nazis and yet the latter were the able ones - the very ones who knew how to govern and who seemed to be essential and to be used by the occupying powers.

THE TEAM'S WORK

Unit 4

From September 1946 Unit 4 operated from the town of Schleswig. The work covered the area from the Kiel canal to the Danish border, from the islands of Sylt, Föhr and Amrum in the

west, to the Baltic in the east, an area whose main industry had been the breeding of cattle. The population of the island of Sylt was formerly 7,000. Now, with expellees it was 28,000. To supervise and help in the 200 camps in this vast area of Schleswig the team relied on 4 cars, 2 trucks, one ambulance and two lorries. They travelled some 12,000 miles a month and along terribly bad roads, often impassable with sand or snow or floods. The team moved to more

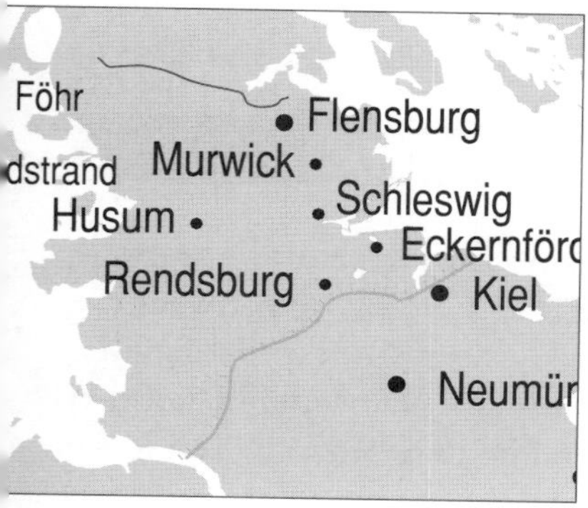

Map labels: Föhr, Flensburg, dstrand, Murwick, Schleswig, Husum, Eckernförd, Rendsburg, Kiel, Neumür

spacious accommodation in March '47 - a great advantage for unpacking and repacking Red Cross and CARE parcels, Arctic and Pacific Packs.

Expellees would arrive at a camp with whatever they had been able to assemble in perhaps ten minutes, and carry or push, on a journey which may have lasted from 7 to 15 days without proper provisions. Valuables and warm clothing were frequently stolen en route. Some old people and children would expire on arrival. From the trains they had been directed into the first transit camp, where they were de-loused and registered; then moved on at once to regional transit camps for three days of full medical examinations, treatment for scabies, sometimes for dysentery. Then they arrived at their billet or at their permanent camp in a land which was strange and different from the home they had left, and among a people temperamentally different.

Most of the work was done through the German welfare organisations. Clothing from Red Cross stores, or sent from Britain as a result of appeals by writing to the papers, was transported to the welfare centres for distribution. Special food was delivered for the child feeding schemes in 91 out of the 200 camps. German staff selected 10 out of every 100 children who were given a hot drink every two days, the food being prepared and consumed on the spot. Practical help was given in convalescent camps for children, in Old People's homes, Disabled Soldiers' homes, orphanages, maternity homes and Kindergartens.

Taped Recollections

Margaret Slee (Unit 4)

UNDESERVED REWARDS

We did not really deserve the thanks for the penicillin we were able to get and deliver. Nor was the great joy we got when we took children back, really deserved. Inevitably, expellee families often became separated on the journey. We would be notified that there would be a batch of children to collect and "Could we see if we could find their parents?" We understood that it might be in the village of So-and-so that they had been settled. And you'd have these kids in the back of your ambulance, and our own German was pretty limited. But you'd make what soothing remarks you could. Having found these isolated hamlets you would knock on doors to try to find people of the right name; and hoped to goodness you were getting the right ones. I can remember knocking on the door of one such place, and the people inside coming rather suspiciously to the door, seeing what appeared to be a British military vehicle, and somebody in khaki - you know. And then you explained haltingly that you had some children and you understood one of them might possibly be related to somebody there. And the appearance from the house of two or three battered-looking refugees, who then burst upon these children with cries of amazement and joy, and everybody embracing everybody else and after signing a couple of chits you drove away thinking, well, you know, that's somebody back where they belong.

SCRAP

One interesting and exciting day we discovered a disused German aerodrome in Husum, a repository for smashed-up planes. I can remember the RAF man at the gate raising the pole that allowed us in, and in we went, the whole unit together - 12 vehicles. We hared across to where these planes were - hundreds of them all tipped up at rakish angles - and just let rip. We set about these planes like maniacs with hammers and crowbars, tearing off sheet duralumin, dismantling tyres, loading anything that was going to be turned into something useful for the refugee camps - loading till the vehicles were bursting at the seams. I know I stayed so long hacksawing, chiselling, tearing off with bare hands, that night came on and I could still hear bangs and clatters till I realised it wasn't the rest of the team still working, it was the wind rising through broken bits of plane that were just chattering in the wind. Everyone else had gone. Anyhow, we dumped all this stuff at our depot, and then Allan [Page] set up workshops in the camps wherever he could and with the skill that many refugees had, they converted the tyres into rubber soles for children's shoes, and the metal beaten and fastened into cans and boxes and containers and cooking pots and so on. It kept them going for a few months.

THE DUMP

The first time I drove a 5-ton lorry was when we drove to a depot where there was a stack of German uniforms and other materials which they had surrendered. One room was full of jack-knives (which had useful things like tin-openers on them). Another was full of boots — thousands of them, in good condition too, but not tied together in pairs. Imagine the heartbreak of having all these and not being able to match them up. All we could do was to dump a load on a camp and say "See what you can find". But the uniforms they could cut up for children's clothing — it was good cloth.

MAKING BUREAUCRACY WORK, TOO

An ex-RAF mess in Flensburg had lain unused for some months. It had been requisitioned by an RAF Officer of a certain rank. We discovered it and although it had been neglected (the pipes had burst and the heating system was kaput) realised its potential for the benefit of refugees; but an approach to the RAF was frustrating - no officer could be found with sufficient interest or seniority. So, after months of this, Stan got to work at the top. He explained the situation to Admiral Bevan and asked him how his rank compared with the requisitioning Officer's. "Oh, said the Admiral, I outrank him" and he signed a de-requisitioning Order and arranged for the buildings to be made available to us. Its first use was as a base for an international work camp with German volunteers included - a traditional SCI "pick and shovel" type scheme: fuel cutting for an old people's home. Because food for Germans was so scarce we begged all the volunteers from abroad, Switzerland, Sweden, Holland, Denmark, to bring as much food as they could carry; but the army helpfully classified us as "Forces Families", so in the end the work-camp had good rations. After the work camp, the building was to be used for a refugee children's home.

THE TEAM'S WORK (CONTINUED)

The team set up an exhibition of the camp workshop crafts. It was displayed in Schleswig, Flensburg and Westerland (Sylt). It created much interest and had an influence on local trade and industry afterwards.

Other initiatives were the carpet factory and travelling library on Sylt; the spinning and weaving and knitting of woollen goods from wool donated from abroad; encouraging women's meetings for discussions and for sewing and patching, and then persuading British Service men's wives to join them; getting refugees to help other refugees by darning and patching for children's homes; encouraging the organising of camp entertainments.

Team members organised regular adult discussion groups, international in nature, which proved quite a rich field for disagreement with the occupation authorities. They arranged talks in schools, pen-friendships abroad, and for English schools to adopt schools and children's homes in the Flensburg camps.

Youth work had quite far-reaching effects, continuing as it did long after the team left, in the local Internationaler Zivildienst (IZD - German version of IVSP), with some 40 members in Schleswig and other groups in Rendsburg, Kiel and, together with Danish relief workers, in Eckernförde. There was a week-long work-camp at Westerland (Sylt). Team members helped in 14 week-end work-camps, working on children's playgrounds, clearing waste land, dismantling air-raid shelters; and stump-grubbing for fuel for old people's and children's homes. A youth group (18-25) started in September '47. It made wooden toys, shoes, and knitted goods and needlework.

Constant appeals for needles, cotton and material for patching, for old clothes, even food, to friends in Britain resulted in a steady stream of these invaluable treasures which did much for camp morale, and enabled many more people to become involved in this work of reconciliation: Oxfam responded with a special grant of £100, for example; and special mention should be made of Jim Legge in the London office, who devoted so much time trying to supply the teams' needs from Britain. He even managed to track down the right sort of bicycle chain to enable a German midwife to resume her mobility and thus her work on her bicycle.

Taped Recollections

MS

"TAKE THIS LOT"

One of the more joyful things that we had was when supplies became available we took them round rather like Father Christmas. I can remember once - it was just before Christmas — every other member of the unit had finished delivering and I was still out in Kreis Husum with some bales of material in the back of my ambulance. It was snowing and many side roads were already blocked, but what was the good of taking the stuff back to base when people were needing it? So, on the way home when I came across a village and if there was anyone about I stopped them and said: "Look, are there any needy children in this area?" And when they gave me some information I would say: "Take this lot. See what you can do with it." And the joy that you could create was beyond belief.

ALL IN A GOOD CAUSE

We operated in Schleswig from the North Sea to the Baltic and so reliable transport was vital. When the need arose we had to go to Bremen for vehicles and spares. Stan indented for a replacement ambulance and parts and I set off with him to collect the order from Bremen.

We followed the army signs and discovered that the depot was a long stretch of disused and deserted autobahn. Parked army trucks of all sizes lined the route as far as you could see. We called at the control office and Stan chatted to the Sergeant in charge as we signed for our order. He then asked if there were any spare tilts - one of ours being so decrepit we could no longer use the lorry for refugee supplies.

The Sergeant was sympathetic but said he had no authority to release one. More appeals from Stan; and then the Sergeant: "Well, look. The trucks along there are all listed but the tilts haven't been booked in yet. Need I say more?" Rejoicing, we lost no time in driving merrily along the route for a mile or more until we found a lorry neatly fitted with a good new tilt. "That's ours!" said Stan.

We pulled in behind the lorry. Stan went to undo the ropes on the offside and I climbed up the nearside. We were busy, happily throwing the ropes down and dragging off the huge tarpaulin, when I saw far distant a jeep racing our way. "Look out, Stan! I called, what do we do?" He looked. "Carry on, he said, with any luck he'll think we're entitled to it, and pass on." We did, but the jeep pulled up with a squeal of brakes and out jumped the OC Depot himself, shouting "What the hell do you think you're doing?"

Blandly, rolling up the last bit, Stan explained that the Unit's stores were suffering because of our rotted equipment, and it seemed an excellent opportunity to remedy the situation. The Officer, red in the face, expostulated furiously, ending by telling us to put it back, and observing that if our CO had requested one earlier it could have been a different matter.

To my amazement I heard Stan, after acknowledging that our action was irregular, repeat the Unit's urgent need and said "If you would have let us have one on indent, now we've taken one off, can't we take it back with us anyway?" I thought the OC would explode. He was incoherent and then shouted "Take it! But your CO will hear of this." and he roared away in the jeep.

"Quick! said Stan, let's get it into the ambulance fast. I must get back before he contacts 109 (our Unit)- or HQ!" We did, and as soon as we were back at Moltkestrasse he phoned Bremen Vehicle Park.

"Hello, says he to our apoplectic officer, I believe one of my unit has brought back a tilt that had not been requested. I *do* apologise. It's quite true ours has disintegrated, but that's no excuse. I've sent for the man, of course, and given him a rocket he'll not forget in a hurry. I'll have the tilt sent back at once." "That's all right, old boy, said the Major, keep it. We all know this sort of thing goes on. He was just unlucky I caught him out!"

CONTRASTS

MS

15.3.47 *Murwick has two hundred typhus cases and urgently needs extra medical and food supplies. Allan and I got to the Frauen Klinik and loaded doctors' gowns and feeding bottles into the ambulance, but the Flensburg road was still blocked (with snow). I tried again alone on Thursday but the road was blocked with great Danish lorries stuck in drifts, so with one girl I'd picked up I turned and set off back to Schleswig. Old tracks were obliterated by new powdery snow, each drift deeper than the last. We rocked the ambulance through a hundred yards of drift and took to spades. The snow was fine as dust ... it was scarcely possible to breathe ... we had to dig first the windward rut, tossing the clouds of powder to the centre, then clear that low enough for the axle to pass, and hurl the snow out of the second rut, and charge and rock into the filling hollows. Roadmen told us the road was blocked for miles with drift-bound vehicles. So we carried the supplies to a cottage, where the girl stayed, and I set off in a swirl of smoke-like snow 15km south for Schleswig on foot.*

6.4.47 *On the way back from Nordstrand, over the broken road into the edge of a forested rise the road swings suddenly through a pine belt, and bright against the dark woods shines the Kreis Crest of Husum, its gold boat rocking on a scarlet sea. Following a marshy path out of the cold wind into the forest, found no flowers but thick patches of vivid moss, pink and white ... birches, rosy alder catkins with spruce and silver fir. Two young deer bounded into view, wide-eyed, graceful, their swift passing scarcely broke the silence as their tiny hooves flashed through the brake from the marsh edge.*

*I.V.S.P. lorry, loaded with supplies for Flensburg refugee camps, stuck in the snow –
Margaret Slee unloaded full load into cottage and walked back to Schleswig. Great
cold winter of 46 - 47 – and no wellingtons!*

SNAPSHOT - RECREATION

HWR (Unit 4)

At our party just after Christmas 1946 were our German friends,
interpreters and others involved with our work. Also with us were
two Don Suisse, Gerti Oehler and Ruth Baltensperger, the
vanguard of the team coming from Kleve to Kiel. The usual games
of a mildly competitive nature were played and the results
announced in typical British manner. A lady interpreter turned to
me in surprise saying: "Whoever heard of three cheers for the
losers!"

FINNMARK

EN ROUTE FOR THE ARCTIC CIRCLE

I had a pleasant afternoon out with Ingrid the Norwegian tutor whom I took round to Guide HQ as she was extremely interested. The G.I.S. Chairwoman & Deputy both of whom I met in Germany gave me a terrific welcome and have promised to forward any needed supplies for us to distribute in Finnmark.

We had a 1-day conference last Sunday to discuss the future of IVSP but got little past arguing on whether our purpose was the witnessing to a belief or general conversion. Derek, John & I argued that one really efficiently run scheme was of much more ultimate value than six schemes lacking in efficiency even though six times as many people were thus associated with the movement. By all means publish a report but make it a portrayal of the work and present the motive behind it without making a pressing appeal for volunteers.

Letter, 21/5/46, FJM to Alastair.

I had to address an IVSP meeting in the afternoon. It went very well indeed and we discussed in some detail the inclusion of ex-Nazis in schemes with the group having rather varied ideas. Strangely enough Marcia Kallman whom you saw in London was the most broad-minded despite the fact that she was brutally tortured and was the chief witness at the prosecution of the Norwegian N.S. lad who did it. (She felt bad about this but Ingrid & she visited him in his cell afterwards and they left no personal animosity between them.) We have heard that our visit has put new life into IVSP as until our arrival it was not very active — the members having resumed their studies etc. (but who can blame them?)

SWITZERLAND
[1946]

DLS

[These entries were made at an SCI Conference of National Secretaries and others at the Herzberg, Aarau, near Zurich, and during subsequent weeks in NW Germany]

Tuesday June 4. *Basel at last (having received some petrol from the French at Freiburg) after a hold-up of half-an-hour or so at the frontier, owing, regrettably, to my papers not being in order. They were obtained specially for me for this journey by HQ5 at Vlotho & notwithstanding were dated so as to be invalid when I arrived. However, an extension was granted, and having been relieved of our Reichsmarks & given a receipt we proceeded, buying some unrationed petrol with Francs (provided by Miss Roberts in Basel) on the way.*

Herzberg was reached in one, having chosen the right way, but, alas, the regulator went kaputt on the journey & the battery will not now be charging. Hoffentlich it will last until we get back. If not, there are plenty of hills here to start on. I had supper and met some new friends as well as old. Discussion of tomorrow's programme & so to bed, in a wooden building high up on a hillside overlooking Aarau which is visible far beneath through the V of two neighbouring wooded hillsides. 430 km & new faces & meetings sent me tired to the attic.

Wednesday June 5. *The first session of the conference was informal, and sometimes in French, sometimes German and sometimes English. Just before lunch I looked at the sky to the south and thought how like mountains the clouds were, and was startled to hear Willi ask if I saw the mountains.*

Sunday June 9. *A walk with Ernst Wolf before breakfast was a good start. At lunch I had a tête-à-tête with Madeleine Jécquier about her* *friends in Germany, the situation there & present doubts in Switzerland about the Fellowship of Reconciliation as not being very practical. And a talk with Magda Zingg & Jenny Meister & Alice Brugger. More talk after lunch, with many people beginning to be rather on edge - Hans & Theo played truant. I was called on to describe in German the work in Germany but was permitted after a minute or two of hard work to continue in English. Bernard Klausner contributed to the discussion on Germany & impressed by his grasp of the principles and his way of presenting them.*

The impressions made by the people at the Swiss conference were fairly striking. The ablest person there was I think undoubtedly <u>Donald Bentley</u>. His opinion was received with great respect & he often settled a question to everybody's satisfaction almost without further discussion. The advantages of being able to be witty in both French & English are of course tremendous & he also frequently enlivened the proceedings by a sly dig or a particular intonation when reading Minutes. I realised as I had done in England how much Donald has meant to the development of the movement.

<u>Willy Begert</u> was at the conference to get his orders, so to speak, & did not therefore take a very leading part in the discussions. As this was the first time I'd met him, therefore, I can't say that he is not the equal or superior of Donald. His technical qualifications are at least impressive. He speaks English, French, German, Swizzer-Tuetsch (Swiss-German), Danish, Spanish, Greek. He has had varied experience in all these countries. He also has a highly-developed sense of humour. He has a curious appearance - tall & thin, with a rugged, brown face, longish jaw & high cheekbones, a squint, and long unkempt dark hair. At the conference he usually wore white socks. He told us that in Greece he was driving once in a truck with a Greek interpreter & passed two old women with bundles of wood. He stopped to give them a lift, & by the time he got round to the back of the truck, the interpreter had got the back down & the bundles of wood on, but as he appeared they looked at one another, held a hurried consultation, & took the wood off the truck again, preferring to walk. And one old man in a camp used to

cross himself each time he saw Willy. He has an extensive acquaintance with English sea songs, & can talk & sing till the cows come home, & frequently much later.

Ralph Hegnauer, the Swiss Secretary, is another of the business men with a firm & practical grasp of the details of the movement as well as of the principles. A fairly young man with a varied career behind him & now a shop which his wife looks after, he gives all his time to the secretaryship. He speaks a curiously clipped & precise & clearly enunciated French & German & occasionally cannot find a word in the language he happens to be speaking & replaces it from the other. I was told he is sometimes difficult to work with, & can imagine that that is so, but he works extraordinarily hard & well for the Swiss Branch & was a valuable member of the conference. We got on very well, & he was to the fore in our "party" & on the evenings when bowls were played.

Pierre Martin I had heard of before, not very favourably, from Alastair McLaren. He was however a very pleasant, quiet young man, constantly smiling, with a round face & black hair brushed straight back from the forehead, & round dark glasses when the sun was strong. He has had an unpleasant career during the war, in prison & forced labour camps. His organising ability seems to lack something, however, and Donald was not altogether happy about the French Branch's schemes.

Henri Roser, a middle-aged pastor, officer in the last war, in prison as a pacifist in this, the Vice-Chairman of the French Branch, carried with him an atmosphere of cheerfulness & steadiness. He is a big man (with, like Willy, a squint) & carries himself well. I have seen him deadly earnest in developing a point of principle, wistful, humorous, and playing games like a boy, laughing helplessly. One would call him a good man.

Albert Ueltschi, President of the Swiss Branch, a French-speaker, is middle-aged. Hans after a day or two said to me "Isn't he a nice man?" - he was friendly & fatherly. His French was sometimes stammering and seemed rapid, though really it was very irregular in speed. He sometimes put lengthy queries which were based on a misconception of what someone had said (the languages used varying with remarkable rapidity) & had some individual ways of putting things - eg he always referred to Ethelwyn (& others, but it seemed most curious in E's case) as "Notre amie Best". He doodled during the conference in a particularly competent way, producing botanical drawings of some skill, and he constantly kept his pencils properly pointed & performed the like office for those sitting next to him.

GERMANY (II)
(1946)

PRE-WAR THREADS

There must have been many German volunteers in SCI camps since the start of the movement in 1920, but it still seemed rather miraculous that after the Hitler years at least four of them identified themselves to IVSP team members: Walter Koch, mentioned on page 6 of the IVSP History, Walter Thieleman who helped organise the Köhlbrand (Hamburg) work-camp in the summer of 1946; and also from Hamburg a housewife, Carlotta von Pavel; and in Münster, Prof. Förste.

JOURNAL – CONTINUED

Monday June 17 *Went into Münster to see Dr. Koch about tomorrow's conference & found that he had everything arranged.*

Tuesday June 18 *With Anneliese who arrived overnight with Ian, to Münster, to the Oberpraesidium, where we met Dr. Koch, Joachim, & others. The conference started about 9.25 & finished about 11.35, & it was two hours well spent, with a fairly international & representative gathering - there were 3 Britishers, 1 Swiss, 1 Bulgarian - a Doctor who has been lecturing in Hamburg for some time - & the rest Germans. A youngish man introduced himself as Prof. Förste of Münster University, who had served with IVSP at Rhos in North Wales, & Walter Thieleman from Hamburg, another well-known IVSP member was there.*

Friday June 28 *The journey to Hamburg was uneventful. I stopped for a cup of tea at a Mobile Canteen near Soltau & met there two Scouts, one of whom had been in Greece & knew Willy Begert very well.*

I contacted the Salvation Army in Hamburg & found out where I was to be accommodated, whither I was guided by two Guides in a two-seater.

They have just arrived as a Guide training team & are also working with Baltic D.P.s, & I mentioned the IVSP schemes in case there's any interest in that sphere.

I found myself in a hotel again — Officer's Transit Hotel (Streit's Hotel) — in Room 109 (coincidence in team number) with its own bathroom & a previous occupant of the second bed who from the evidence is here for some time. I have not yet met him face to face, but he seems to be a Lieutenant in some peculiar regiment whose sign is a harp, whether Welsh, Irish, Canadian/Irish or a regiment of the Army of the Lord I don't know.

Found Walter Thieleman (who is one of the 50,000 or so who are to be turned out of a section of the city to provide accommodation for the Control Commission for Germany) & had some talk with him, went to Frau v. Pavel's to find her out, and thence to Dr. Michaltscheff with whom we discussed arrangements for tomorrow.

Dinner at the hotel, opposite an UNRRA girl, Canadian, on the way to London for leave. Found a message at the desk to phone Barbara Travers tomorrow morning at HQ5; why, I wonder.

Slight preparation for my talk to some young people (arranged by Frau v. Pavel) tomorrow evening, hot bath (in own bathroom), & bed.

Saturday June 29 And, by gum, it was a hot bath. Having turned on the tap I got ready for the bath & when I went back, after quite a short time, the thing was full; and a deep bath it was too. It had to be cooled considerably & by that time & with me in it the water came very near the top, & I noticed a tendency to float. Extravagance is easy.

Met Walter & Dr. M. outside the hotel at 8.30 & then spent half an hour getting a dock pass to take us through the Elbe Tunnel, a very considerable short cut to our destination (Köhlbrand). We were held up again however at the last stage of our journey when we had to wait for a ferry, & as we had to catch the same ferry on the return journey our time for looking round the site of the scheme was rather too limited. However, we went over the place which is along the water side and consists of a number of buildings, mostly wooden, in which before the war about 3000 children used to be looked after daily, being brought in the morning and taken back at night. Now it is only possible to accommodate 500, because it's had a bomb & has also been neglected so that sand has accumulated to a considerable depth over the site. There seems to be the possibility of a very good IVSP scheme there.

We got back through the docks — damaged everywhere, of course — in good time, tried to see the Education Officer, Mr. Horsnell, who was however out; and having deposited Walter, had a few minutes with the Rector of the University, Professor Dr. Emil Wolff, [a famous English scholar] who is interested in the IVSP schemes & said he would visit the one at Köhlbrand.

Phoned HQ5 & learned that the Col. has OKed the call forward of extra people. Wrote to Derek with this information & other, & did some other typing.

In the afternoon, I picked up Dr. M. & Walter again & took them to Frau v. Pavel's where we met Herr v. P. & Herr Ressing, the journalist who was at our Münster conference. A long conversation ensued on the relations between Germans & the British Occupying Forces in which pros & cons were put by the circle (I listened without taking part) with a good deal of objectivity, though there was a feeling of exasperation at some of the lack of positive guidance & intention, especially when there is no information available; and an inability to understand some of the things that are done or the reason for doing them or for preventing them from happening.

Eventually we discussed the practical matters concerning the Köhlbrand scheme; and on the way back called on Frau Kröger, a Quaker, whom Dr. M. invited to tomorrow's meeting.

Had a very hasty meal & went off again to Herr Ressing's house where I arrived after chasing my tail for some minutes in an effort to find the location.

We had a very interesting evening - the room was full (about 30 people there) mostly of young people, half a dozen of whom were girls, & there were several Britishers: Lt. Goodland who is concerned with Youth work in Hamburg, an officer of the Information Control Unit, a civilian Mil. Gov. officer of German origin, a sergeant & myself. I opened the proceedings with an introduction on IVSP (in English, with some extracts from 'literature' in German) & after a few questions the discussion developed into a general one on youth problems, the issue of a Youth Newspaper — for which there is not yet enough paper — the possibility of interchange of young people between countries, & so on. It went on till 11 when the meeting had to break up because of the curfew. A Herr Doering was there from Hamburg Radio, & he arranged to try to get a talk between some British & some German young people over the radio on August 1, which they are holding as Peace day. The Editor of Die Welt

(Herr Ressing's paper) was also there, & made some useful contributions from a knowledge of the facts of the situation.

PERSONALITIES

Took farewell of my room-mate at 8 o'clock this morning [July 1], he just waking. He turned out to be a quite young lieutenant in the 8th Hussars, called something like Brookfield; a pleasant & capable young man, taking after his parents, I judge, whose photographs were on the dressing table - both with round spectacles & beaming smiles, of youngish middle-age & respectable middle-class - a cheerful pair who have made a comfortable little home for themselves & brought up their children (child?) with ambitions for them. The young Mr. Brookfield (if such was his name) is certainly getting on. He was a member of the War Crimes Court which has been sitting in Hamburg - I wonder if it's usual to have such young officers on them.

<u>Dr. Koch</u> is a grand person, with a strong character based on a religious faith, very modest & almost retiring in manner, but not the sort of person you could overlook for long. One of his sons, I was interested to learn, is producer of the Hannover theatre & is at present in Hamburg producing a Shakespeare season (The Tempest) after a successful presentation of Sophocles' Antigone.

<u>Dr. Theodore Michaltscheff</u> is a pacifist in the English sense & gets regular supplies of Peace News & PPU literature for distribution. He is a photographer of considerable ability, & teaches Bulgarian language in the University. He has a mop of curly hair, dark but going slightly grey, which gives his head a bushy appearance, particularly as his features are not regular. His face in repose is a little dreamy, perhaps a little like an ancient Greek philosopher - not, however, so ugly as Socrates! - but he smiles readily and talks sense. He speaks excellent English & converses readily, though in general discussion he does not put himself forward much.

<u>Karl-Heinz Ressing</u> is a youngish man, thin, with hollow cheeks & slightly greying hair - plenty of it - brushed straight back.   He is an animated talker with very sound ideas & a quality of leadership which might be sufficient to hold young people.   He has projects of his own - a Youth Page for the paper, & so on - & puts his ideas into practice - eg last night's meeting, which was to get together German young people along with representatives of the British Forces & people so that questions could be asked and answered & discussion take place in a realistic milieu;   and the Köhlbrand scheme which falls in with his ideas & which he is actively supporting, both in the paper (his Editor has given him more or less carte blanche for that) & in the practical work.   A very good lad.

<u>Walter Thielemann</u> is throwing himself into the work for this scheme with great enthusiasm.   He is a strange man in some ways, the strangeness seeming to come from a nervous energy, though I am surprised to deduce that, because on first meeting & still, in a company of other people, he strikes one as having no particular interest in life & as not being a very active man.   But he talks, when once he starts, rapidly, occasionally stumbling over himself, & often repeating a phrase rapidly, either while he thinks of the next one or because he finds it difficult to come to an abrupt stop.   In the car, he puts off the hand-brake for me as soon as he gets in, switches the indicator to show me as well as the general public which way to go;   and in walking he bustles.   He does not walk well - he has a limp - but he keeps going, goes in front with a "Geh' mal vor" ("I'll go ahead" - apology for going in front of one, usually when it's the sensible thing to do because he knows the way), & when we were going round Köhlbrand trotted us round, pointing out & discussing, or talking to the caretaker in rapid German which mostly escaped me.   He expects to leave his job at the end of July (I don't know why) & is placing himself at the disposal of the scheme for a month & possibly for the whole time.

EXPLAINING IVSP TO GERMANS

**Monday July 1**   I had lunch with Dr. Michaltscheff, who is a vegetarian, & who had managed, with his landlady, Mme Tuczynska, to put on a more elaborate repast than usual for my benefit - we had soup, with some sort of greens in it - whether orthodox vegetable or nettle leaves I don't know, potatoes & runner beans (grown by himself in a window-box), & semolina-blancmange with strawberries.   Excellent.

After lunch people for the meeting began to arrive, & about 25 all told attended, representatives from the German Peace Society, the Quakers, the Fellowship of Reconciliation, the Esperanto Society, the Women's International League for Peace and Freedom, and others.   I dilated once more on IVSP & after some discussion & questions, & a slight tussle with the lady from the Women's League who had a very proper but impracticably extremist anti-Nazi phobia & asked for guarantees that no Nazi could ever come on service, we dispersed after support had been given by all the representatives, including promises of financial assistance.

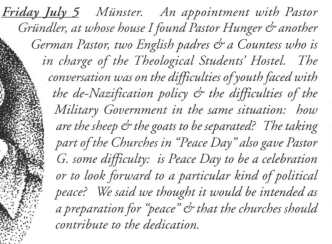

**Friday July 5**   Münster.   An appointment with Pastor Gründler, at whose house I found Pastor Hunger & another German Pastor, two English padres & a Countess who is in charge of the Theological Students' Hostel.   The conversation was on the difficulties of youth faced with the de-Nazification policy & the difficulties of the Military Government in the same situation: how are the sheep & the goats to be separated?   The taking part of the Churches in "Peace Day" also gave Pastor G. some difficulty: is Peace Day to be a celebration or to look forward to a particular kind of political peace?   We said we thought it would be intended as a preparation for "peace" & that the churches should contribute to the dedication.

An I.V.S.P. volunteer

DARKNESS & LIGHT

SECOND KÖHLBRAND WORK-CAMP

Norman Lancashire (Unit 7)

While with the Duisburg team, I spent a couple of weeks in 1946/ 47 at the work camp at Köhlbrand on the Elbe, Hamburg, where we volunteers shovelled sand back on to the river beach, from which the wind had blown it. This was to re-instate a children's holiday centre there.

After the evening meal each day were the usual sing-songs and talks. Two or three young Germans of both sexes described how they had helped as auxiliaries on the anti-aircraft batteries in Hamburg - the widespread ruins of which we had all seen so recently. They had had their suppers, done their school homework, and then the British bombers had come over. Oddly enough, the Germans called the RAF "Tommies" - "Die Tommyflieger".

These volunteers had strange stories to tell. Many more bombers were probably shot down than BBC news claimed. They dropped their bombs, sometimes machine-gunned the AA batteries, but often, said these young Germans, a bomber would be hit and forced to crash-land, whereupon. all at once, there would be a transformation, both rôles of attacker and defender would be abandoned. They spoke of rushing to the scene when a plane was coming down on fire, and they tried to rescue the air crew. However, because of the heat, the escape hatch had jammed. When finally they quelled the flames and succeeded in prising open the door, they found all the crew were crowded behind it - dead - where they had been desperately trying to escape, also unable to open the door.

This was one of several similar stories. Some were gruesome enough. A bomber had landed, burning, and could not be approached at first. Again, the crew were found dead inside, but when they pulled one crew member out by his leg, it stretched horrifically because of the effect of the heat. Nevertheless, many of their rescue attempts were successful in saving airmen's lives.

ST. STEPHAN, SWITZERLAND

In 1947, working in another pick-and-shovel work camp, I was given another perspective of the war in the air. Swiss IVSP volunteers had seen the RAF and US Air force occasionally bomb Zürich and Bern by mistake, being fired on, and not always noticing the Swiss white-on-red crosses on the fighter planes sent up against them. Sometimes, shattered RAF bombers would lose their way after bombing Germany, navigational instruments shot to pieces, and the Swiss anti-aircraft units would still open up on them as they groped their way home.

We were even given an alleged eye-witness account of refugees trying to cross into Switzerland, being refused entry by the Swiss frontier guards, even with German soldiers hard on their heels. When turned back, the fugitives were not only captured, but actually beheaded in full view of the Swiss.

Yet at the very end of the war, when the Dutch - particularly the children - in one area were suffering near starvation, the RAF came to a temporary agreement with the Germans (which was honoured) that they would be allowed safe passage for transports to parachute in food and sweets.

So, humane feelings were, one feels ... likes to hope ..., always ready to break through.

Taped Recollections

MS (Unit 4)

BROUGHT UP SHORT

As new members going to join a team with a year's experience, we were prepared, theoretically at least, for the dreadful conditions we would find in Germany. We expected we would have to be sleeping in tents with very poor and limited equipment. In fact on our way out in April 1946 we found ourselves travelling first class with officer status, like VIPs, from the Hook of Holland into Germany. We were just settling down to this when waiters came round saying that breakfast was being served. So we went along to the dining car with its tables in white damask and silverware. when the train drew up into our first German station. It must have been about 6 am. It was an absolute blow in the face. There was the platform packed solid with grey drab figures, hungry-looking, and miserable, trying to keep warm, waiting for hours for trains that never came. And there we were like trapped zoo specimens sitting in luxury and feeding on bacon and egg and toast and marmalade. while they stared silently at us. My appetite vanished. I thought: "This is not what we came here for. We came to help."

WHAT'S TO COME IS STILL UNSURE

Leslie Gore (Unit 7)

The team of which I was a member gathered in London in January 1946. We were unknown to each other: our ages ranged from 24 to 45; our interests and beliefs were similarly diverse. A hectic round of lectures, buying equipment, enduring inoculations, and sewing on Red Cross "flashes", left little time for reflection before departure.

Travel spelt transit camp for anyone, civilian or otherwise, caught in the slow shuffle of Army Movement Control, and I subsequently came to reserve a particular kind of dislike for these impersonal halfway houses of identical furniture.

We crossed the Rhine in the early hours of a raw, January morning. Most of us were silent and still, chilled not only by a night in an unheated train but perhaps by our thoughts. It was misty; already we seemed to feel that clammy air of lifelessness which now hung over Germany and with which we were later to become so familiar - a creepy, unreal feeling that sometimes pervaded the atmosphere in which we worked. We started-and-

stopped-and-started our way into Emmerich where breakfast was
served in what had at one time been a school.   Outside was a
bombed and ruined city, with rubble piled high in the streets, and
children begging for food.   Inside was warmth, laden tables,
spotless cutlery, white-coated waiters and - crowning incongruity
- a string quartet.   I shall always retain a picture of those four
men, elderly, respectably dressed, playing as though we were taking
afternoon tea in the Winter Gardens at Bournemouth.   They
played a haunting French café melody, "J'attendrai", sensuous.
pathétique and yet morbid in its melancholy.   At the end one of
their number joined the waiter in a careful collection of cigarette
ends from the ash-trays.

Vlotho, a pleasant little country town on the banks of the
Weser, was the HQ of the British Red Cross under whose capacious
umbrella we, as members of a voluntary society, worked.   We
learnt there that our destination was to be Kevelaer in the
Niederrhein and that our particular task was to concern ourselves
with the Welfare of the German people, through the establishment
of their own voluntary societies, particularly in the towns of Goch,
Geldern and Cleve, which were all classified by military
cartographers as 80% destroyed.   The work of the team in the
next few months resolved itself into the distribution of medical
supplies, instruments, drugs and food to hospitals;   the
establishment of child-feeding and scabies clinics; the distribution
of clothing through "make-do-and-mend" centres, church groups
and orphanages, and the distribution of small supplies of
educational material and youth club equipment, using wherever
possible the channels of existing voluntary societies.

Kevelaer had been by-passed by German and Canadian
Armies and was relatively an oasis of brick and stone in a desert of
destruction. It was the centre of a predominantly Roman Catholic
area, and in previous years pilgrims came from all over Germany
to pray at its shrine.   There were no pilgrims now, and the shops
that had sold them souvenirs and trinkets were closed and
shuttered.   The cafés remained, but these were now frequented
by displaced persons from a nearby camp (which contained thirty

different nationalities), and listless demobbed young Germans. Returned jobless PoWs mingled with Spaniards at one particular cafe - Spaniards who, as political refugees, had been interned in France in the mid-thirties, and later brought to the forced-labour camps of Germany. All drank the same ersatz abominable beer.

It was in one of these cafés that I met Paul. He spoke an Americanised English, having been for some months in a special camp in Northern France, for the re-education of young Germans. He was then eighteen years of age, had been a member of the Hitler Jugend and was at sixteen engaged as a member of the Luftwaffe in the manning of anti-aircraft guns on the outskirts of Köln. Later he was called for training in the SS, but the end of the war came before his training was completed. Whether the re-education supplied by the U S Army, or whether his early upbringing prompted the questions in his mind, I know not. Like countless other young Germans at that time he did not know what to believe; that in which he had placed his faith and hopes had tumbled about his ears and he had nothing or very little to put in its place. His parents were devout Catholics and one could see time and time again the struggle which went on in his mind as we talked. On the one hand I was conscious of the influence of his home, modest beside the glory that had been his as a young Nazi; and on the other hand the influence of National Socialism. There were so many like Paul. Some were bitter and quite unapproachable - still National Socialists in all but name. Others took refuge in a cynical nihilism; others were searching. When we were tired of talking we played football. I often think that the real value of the work we did in Germany was achieved not so much through official channels, but through the unofficial things we did.

The Autumn of my stay in Germany was spent in administration. I helped Basil Eastland to arrange a conference of those who had taken part in work camps during the Summer. I visited other Relief Teams. I drove the length and breadth of the autobahn system which in the Ruhr seemed to assume the magic quality of being able to transport one through space. One drove high, leaving the ghastly catacombs of the Ruhr on either side. The Autumn was still and warm, the autobahn clean and deserted; on either side, in contrast, was degradation, dirt, hunger and want; crowded ruins of people engaged in a struggle for survival. I thought of German-occupied France, Belgium, Holland and the rest. Did the "punishment fit the crime"? Who sinned? And who was sinned against? I could not answer.

I left Germany via the now familiar transit camp, and came to the Hook of Holland. The familiar messroom and lounge was there, the same chairs of boxed green leather, the same bar. A young Dutchman played an accordion. We waited. I was dreaming rather than listening until I heard again the strains of the melody which had greeted our arrival in Germany, but the quality was different, the touch lighter, the melody no longer haunting and melancholic, but lilting, calling us to dance. This was Holland, not Germany. A people that had suffered and survived; where there had been death there was now life. It had not yet come to Germany and I wondered if it ever would.

THE LONG ARM

A series of quite remarkable coincidences linking the beginning of SCI with the work of Unit 4 was part of the excitement of that team's work. It started in Utrecht, to which the team had been directed for further orders after leaving Tilburg. Ramsay Bramham, the team leader, had worked with IVSP for several years and had an extensive knowledge of the movement, its origins and principles. He had to go to an Army Transit Officer for a further Movement Order and came back to the team in great excitement. We were to proceed to a billet in Bilthoven. This didn't mean much to most of us, but when Ramsay explained, we understood. In 1920 the International Fellowship of Reconciliation called a meeting to try to find ways of putting the ideal of reconciliation into practice, and the place put at the disposal of the Fellowship for the purpose was 'het Werkplaats', a progressive school founded

Walter Koch (1946/7) kick-started S.C.I. in 1920

in their home by Kees and Betty (Cadbury) Boeke. Among the others who attended were Pierre Ceresole, a Swiss engineer, and a German, Walter Koch. The idea of international work-camps was discussed at length until Walter Koch urged the others to stop talking and get on with it. This was taken up by Pierre Ceresole, who went on to found SCI along with his brother Ernest, not like Pierre a pacifist but a Colonel in the Swiss army.

Kees and Betty Boeke carried on with their school in Bilthoven and during the war gave refuge to Jews, Kees being imprisoned for some time; and like the rest of the Dutch population suffered the added hardship of the Hunger Winter of 1944. For five years Kees and Betty saw no British person, and then in May 1945 a Mr. van Gelder who had had contact with the team suggested to Kees that he might investigate a British team which had come to Bilthoven. Finlay *[p.90]* wrote to his brother Alastair: "On Tuesday [28-5-45] a tall, pleasant individual came up to Bruce and I who were working on the vehicles and started to talk to us and we awaited the customary request for 'fags'. His conversation however took another line and he sought information about IVSP. Being in overalls our Service Civil Vol. Int. flash was not visible otherwise his enquiries would have been unnecessary. You will no doubt have jumped to the conclusion - Here was Kees Boeke the International Secretary of the FoR who called the Conference out of which IVSP originated. You can guess how we felt. The coincidence amazed us." It also profoundly moved Kees.

Early the next year I had to get in touch with the German Minister of Education in the provisional government of Nord-Rhein/Westfalen for approval of and assistance with the arrangements for the international work-camps which were to be organised. This was a Dr. Koch (one of the commonest surnames in Germany) whom I met in his office in Düsseldorf, and to whom I began to explain about IVSP. I had barely started when he smiled a slow smile and said, "I think I know something about this. My brother Walter is a Quaker, and he had something to do with it."

DLS

Letter, 24/2/46, FJM to his family:
The other business [p.118] was a rather strange mission which covers almost the period that we have been in Göttingen. About the first week that we were here David and I visited a Professor who gave us a most interesting account of life under Hitler and how he had listened to the BBC and kept a very incriminating

Diary as a result of an appeal by a Broadcaster. When next Dave visited him he had just been dismissed in an anti-Nazi purge from the 'varsity and while he had spoken at a meeting of the National Socialists in 1936 he had long since thrown over any illusions he had at that time about the possibilities of that regime. He could hardly think that this was the reason yet he could think of no other basis and what made the thing more mysterious was the fact that Field Security had since approached him for information which they wanted from a reliable anti-Nazi source and had called on him because they had got his name from the Gestapo Black List. However to cut a long story short this FRS girl *[Enid Barkas]* was a personal friend of the Prof. as her father had been a colleague of his up to within a fortnight before war was declared and she herself had been a student at Göttingen. We called and got the facts first hand once again and called round at Mil Gov and by way of outdoing all the coincidences of the detective story the man in charge was a family friend of the FRS girl and everything was in the bag though his appeal was about through on its own.

Letter, 21/5/46, FJM (in Oslo) to Alastair.
We went to visit the home of Nansen and while there Halldor phoned asking me if I would like to go to a Party on May 17th as the Red Headed school teacher I had met when speaking to the classes turned out to be a friend of his. Halldor turned up on time as did a Dutch couple who knew Bilthoven well and two student friends of Halldor - all of the three Norges had been at Rosemarkie & were back completing studies. It was a bit of a shock to find some of them in evening dress! It was a bigger shock when 'Red Head' met us and started to 'tick me off' for not having come to see her. This rather staggered me until she explained that she had just received a letter from Maggie Low (the Guide I visited in London) to say she had given me Anna's (the Red Head) address. Can you beat it! Of all the schools in Oslo I go to one where the teacher knows not only a Norwegian but also an English friend in common.

EPILOGUE

UNITED NATIONS RELIEF AND REHABILITATION
ADMINISTRATION, GREECE MISSION
Headquarters - 4 Churchill Street, Athens
BRS/657 2 May 1946

Mr. Willy Begert
International Secretary
Service Civil International
Hilterfingen, Lac de Thoune
Suisse.

My dear Willy,

Apart from any official letters of thanks which may be written by the Chief of Mission to your society, I cannot let you disappear from Greece without sending you a personal message. I think that even your natural modesty cannot have hidden from you what we in the Mission thought of your work. We have certainly been fortunate here in having as allies in our great task a superb series of teams and individuals from various societies. But I can say with absolute truth that amongst such a collection of stars you and your team were outstanding. You were working in an admittedly difficult area which needed most competent handling: and yet we not only never had the slightest doubt as to your success but as you well know wanted to leave those areas in your hands as long as we could.

The whole Welfare Division and certainly I myself are really proud to have worked with you and are deeply grateful for what you did both for us and more particularly for Greece. I hope that at some future time we may meet again to talk over our experiences.

Sincerely yours,
Michael Lubbock
Colonel
Deputy Chief of Mission, Relief Division

The RELIEF TEAMS LEAVE GERMANY

Hamburg-Blankenese
March 29th 1949

When, one fine day in 1946, I found myself in the company of a dozen or so other Hamburg people waiting for the IVSP Advisory Officer *[Senior Representative]*, I hadn't really much of a notion what IVSP stood for. Moreover, when I saw the chap entering the room, wearing a long beard, I did have some slight doubts and suspicions that we had fallen into the hands of a fanatic or a world reformer of some sort. The way, however, our friend talked to us, expounding IVSP's aims and their plans for organising international work camps at Köhlbrand and at other places during the summer months, did make sense; finally, the Köhlbrand service itself more than held what had been promised to us.

From that time on I have been highly privileged to make the acquaintance of many members of the IVSP relief teams. More than once I have been their guest in Berlin, Duisburg and Schleswig, thus getting first-hand glimpses of their work and of their life. I recall one particular night in Berlin during the bitter cold of the winter 1946/47. After a busy day of rushing hither and thither, attending to various jobs and activities, like clothing distribution, student feeding scheme, committee meeting, etc., etc., the "family" sat down rather worn out and listless, for dinner. There wasn't much of a conversation to start with; but by and by they began to report of their work, talking of what they had been able to achieve and of the day's disappointments. The stock of warm clothes for old people and for refugees was rapidly dwindling down; when could new supplies be expected? They would have to try out 20 new recipes for soya flour to determine the best way of using it in child feeding. One member reported that he had "scrounged" so-and-so many rejected tyres from an army unit. Oh, boy, how wonderful! How many pairs of soles for children's shoes would they make and at what earliest possible date could they be collected? The heap of empty cigarette boxes would soon be large enough to be taken to a children's home, to be converted into all sorts of games, houses, railroads, and what not. Before dinner was over, the whole room was seething with energy, new laughing, plans, projects, hopes and fears. Ever since this day this never-tiring spirit of enthusiasm and devotion, in spite of real mountains of material difficulties, human insufficiencies and personal disappointments, has filled my heart with deep gratitude for all those who brought us help, hope and renewed faith in our country's darkest days of misery and prostration. ...

At this moment, when the relief teams of IVSP are withdrawing from Germany, my thoughts are directed in gratitude to what I have come to call a modern miracle. Soon after the war ended, British volunteers left their homes and their jobs to come to the help of people in need and distress in Germany. After some time, they took up work in the Friedland refugee camp near Göttingen. A number of students of Göttingen University had also felt urged to leave their study books for the time being in order to help the old and the sick who kept pouring into Friedland camp from Eastern districts.

Unselfishness, pity and love stirred in the hearts of members of both groups. What was more natural than that these British and German voluntary helpers should meet, and, after some time, agree to combine their strength and their efforts. To the end of the world a good deed will bring forth good results.

Heinrich Carstens

At a re-union in Hannover in 1969 with Adolf Meyer & Hans Temme (ex-Friedlanders), Adolf said that he as a Social Worker & Hans as an Orthopaedic Surgeon often worked together and tried to put into practice in their encounters with people the principles they had learned from SCI at Friedland.

Gerhard Meyer, in a letter to Fred Pitkeathly of June 1993, regrets that he cannot really remember details of the Friedland Workcamp but goes on: "The efforts of you and your friends and fellow-workers had effects not only in building Nissen huts, much more in influencing several of the German students, certainly myself. The experience of this camp had considerable effect on my own thinking". *[Cf. pp 139 - 140]*

Letter to Derek Edwards from W.D.Hogarth, Secretary of COBSRA 1943-7, on receipt of the 'History of IVSP':

Hampstead
31st January 1949

Dear Derek Edwards,

... I do value this book, and your letter, very much indeed. All the time I was in COBSRA I found a special pleasure in working with IVSP because it really did seem to have, as an organisation, a characteristic which I can only describe as being pure in heart. IVSP always seemed to want nothing except to get on with the job in hand; it never took the line that it was doing a favour, or stretching a point, or giving a lead, or in any other way finding outlets for an unsatisfied Ego!

I hope all is going well now with IVSP and with you ...

Yours sincerely,

W.D.Hogarth

UNIT 1 (RRU 4 IVSP)
(Middle East and Greece)

† Willi Begert	leader	
† Ethelwyn Best		EB
Dora Tregenza (Begert-Tregenza)		
Beryl Verling-Brown		
Roy Richards		
Douglas Lascélles		DL
Gerald Prowse		
Huw Birkett		
John Roper	{these three worked for a time	
John Suthren	{as members of a	
Ernest Adames	{"Water Purification Unit"	
Walter Arber		
Cecil Rendle		
Bea Stenhouse	Middle East only	
Irene van Raalte	Middle East only	
Gretel Bluntschli	Swiss SCI	

SENIOR REPRESENTATIVES

† Charles Lindsay	until November 1944	
Godfrey Heaven	from November 1944	GH

UNIT 2 (RRU 13 IVSP)
(Middle East and Crete and Greece)

Derek Maunder	leader	DM
Beatrice Salter		
Bob Allison		
Huw Rees		
Margaret Greenfield (Holgate)		
Reg Brown		
Reuben Say		RRS
Jean Robertson (Roper)		
Joy & Noel Jones		

UNIT 3 (RRU 5 IVSP)
(Middle East and Italy)

† Albert Tomlinson	leader	
† Denys Kay-Robinson	leader after return of Albert	DKR
Ruth Coates		
Lal Hardstone		LH
† Jinny Hardstone		

† Henry (AW) Rablen
Cara Rablen
Phyllis Rate — CR
William B. Thompson — PR
† Hugh Horsfield — WBT
— HH

Later Team Members:

Charles Williams
† Elsa Leman — EL
Frank Jones
Meriol Trevor
Sam Marriage — Seconded from FAU

UNIT 4 (RS 109 IVSP)
Original Team:

† Ramsay Bramham	leader
† Finlay McLaren	dep. leader; to Finnmark (Unit 8) Feb 46 FJM
David Sainty	leader after Ramsay; Senior Rep. from Mar - Aug 46. DLS
Douglas Childs	leader after David
† Stan Slee	leader after Douglas; then BRC Liaison Officer for Westphalia from Apr - Oct 47. SS
† Bruce Harrison	leader of Unit 7 from Jan 46
† Ian Meldrum	
† Fred Pitkeathly	FP
Alan Jessett	BRCS travelling artist from Feb 46
Mary Jessett	
Winifred Roberts	
† Marian Girling	to Rendsburg camp Aug 46

Members of Schleswig Team:

† Stan Slee	leader (see above)
Edith Thompson	arr. Jul 46 leader Apr 47 - Apr 49
† Allan Page	arr. Apr 46 left Oct 48
Sonia King	arr. Jul 46 left Jan 48
Margaret Hickson (Slee)	left Oct 47 MS
Frances Lancashire	left Feb 47
Barry Spear	leader of Unit 4b, left Aug 47
Douglas Treadwell	arr. Jul 46 left Apr 49
Tom Joseph	left May 47
Peggy Milne	from Unit 7 left Apr 49
Norman Smith	from Unit 5 left Aug 47

Later Team Members:

Harry Robertson	from Unit 7 Oct 46 left Jan 47	HWR
† Phyllis Imhof	arr. Jan 47 left Jan 48	
Bill Forse	arr. Jul 47	
Charles Williams	arr. Jun, left Nov 47	
Alan Robertson	from Unit 5 Oct 47 left May 48	
Monica Fear	arr. Nov 47 left Mar 49	
† Jim Tapp	arr. Nov 47 left Mar 49	
Fred Deutsch	arr. Apr 48 left Mar 49	

SENIOR REPRESENTATIVES

David Sainty	Mar to Aug 46
† Basil Eastland	Aug 46 to Oct 48
Bill Bowman	Oct 48 to Mar 49

UNIT 5 (RS 143 IVSP)

Original Team:

† Basil Eastland	leader; Sen. Rep. 21/8/46 - 23/10/48	BE
† Douglas Sowerby	leader after Basil to Nov 46	
Betty Dinwiddy	leader after Douglas to 27/7/48, then IVSP Services Assistant to Feb 49	
† Ewart Stickings	leader of Unit 7 from Jul 46 to Nov 46	
Harry Alcock	to Nov 46; Köhlbrand camp Aug 46	
Jim Budge	to Dec 46; leader of Rendsburg camp Aug 46	
† Reg Champion	to Dec 46; Twisteden camp Aug 46	
Arthur Brown	to Aug 46	
† Jack Penney	to Nov 46	
Margaret Richards		
Catherine Sowerby	to Apr 46	
† Reg Thickens	to Apr 49	

Later Team Members:

Beryl Verling-Brown	
Nan Welsh	
Peggy McLean	
Pegeen Morris	
Bill Bowman	Sen. Rep. from Oct 48
Norman Stanley-Grace	
Alan Robertson	to Schleswig Unit 4 Oct 47
Hans-Peder Pedersen}	
Hans Kryger-Larsen }	from the Danish Peace Movement (Fredsvenners) Apr 47

UNIT 7 (RS 150 IVSP)
Original Team:

† Bruce Harrison	leader (from Unit 4) to Jul 46	
† Ewart Stickings	*ex* Unit 5, leader Jul - Oct 46	
† Charles Balchin	leader from Nov 46 - May 47 then BRCS Liaison for Nieder-Sachsen Jun 47 - Feb 48	CB
Elsie Gainham	leader from May 47	
Donald Hersom	to Apr 47	
Kathleen Morley	to Apr 47	
Eric Rodham	left May 47. Meschede camp, Aug 46	
Elizabeth Mellentin	left Sep 47 thence to Hamburg IAL (Swedish) till Dec 47	
Leslie Gore	left Apr 47 to become IVSP Development Officer and later General Secretary to Feb 49	LG
Eileen Taylor	left l949, thence to DP work until 1963	ET
Peggy Milne	to Unit 4 Mar 46	
Harry Robertson	to Unit 4 Oct 46	
Edith Edwardson		

Later Team Members:

Ralph Cousins	arr Nov 46	
Keith Bywaters		
† Lydia (Bay) Hyde	arr. Aug 46	
Norman Lancashire	arr Nov 46 left 4/47	NL
† Ewart Stickings	from Unit 5, leader after Bruce, from Jul 46	
Monica Clipstone.		

Initials in the right-hand column indicate the volunteers whose reports and recollections have been used in the compilation.

† *Volunteers known to have died.*

ABBREVIATIONS

BRC(S)	British Red Cross (Society)
CA	Civilian Affairs
CARE	American Food Relief parcel
CO	Conscientious Objector (also Commanding Officer, which is not applicable)
COBSRA	Council of British Societies for Relief Abroad
COD	Central Ordnance Depot
DDT	Dichlorodiphenyltrichloroethane: louse powder
DKW	Deutsche Kraftwerke: German make of car
DM	Deutschmark: German currency unit
DP	Displaced Person
EA; EAM	Greek Coalition of the Left
ELAS	Greek Communist-led army
FAU	Friends' Ambulance Unit
FRS	Friends' Service Council
FoR (IFoR)	Fellowship of Reconciliation (International...)
H & S	Hygiene & Sanitation
ID	Identification (Card)
IRC	International Red Cross
IVSP	International Voluntary Service for Peace
KED	Central Distribution Committee in Greece
KKE	Greek Communist Party
Mil Gov	Military Government
ML	Military Liaison
NAAFI	Navy, Army and Air Force Institute
NG	National Guard (Greece)
POW	Prisoner(s) of War
RAMC	Royal Army Medical Corps
RASC	Royal Army Service Corps
RCA	Red Cross Administration
RE	Royal Engineers
Rec	Recreation Ground
Red X	Red Cross
REME	Royal Electrical & Mechanical Engineers
RRU	Relief and Rehabilitation Unit
RTO	Railway Transport Officer
SCF	Save the Children Fund
SCI	*Service Civil International*

TB	Tuberculosis
UK	United Kingdom (Britain)
UNESCO	United Nations Educational Scientific & Cultural Organisation
UNO	United Nations Organisation
UNRRA	United Nations Relief & Rehabilitation Administration
USSR	Union of Soviet Socialist Republics (Russia)
VD	Venereal Disease
VIP	Very Important Person
Vol-Soc	Voluntary Societ/y, /ies
YWCA	Young Womens Christian Association

REFERENCES

Towards A Christian International — *The Story of the International Fellowship of Reconciliation.* [Chapter VII]. Lilian Stevenson. (1929: 3rd edition 1941.) Drayton House, Gordon Street, London.

International Voluntary Service for Peace 1920-1946 A History — Editors: Ethelwyn Best and Bernard Pike. (1948) George Allen & Unwin Ltd. London.

Pierre Ceresole Passionate Peacemaker — Daniel Anet, Tr. and abridged by Marjorie Taylor. (First published Switzerland 1969. Published in English 1974) The Macmillan Co of India Ltd. Madras.

SCI with and for refugees — SCI international secretariat (1964) Zürich.

Grenzen der innovativen gesellschaftspolitischen Arbeit der Freiwilligenorganisation Service Civil International — Katrin Hainke. (December 1995) Unpublished Diplomarbeit for the Technischen Universität Berlin. 94pp + appendices.

The Vale and Gates of Usc-Con. Rev J.E. Gordon Cartlidge FRHistS, Hon CF. Printed by Robert P. Griffiths (1935).

The SCI Archive is held at Bibliothèque de la Ville, Rue de Progrès 33, CH-2305 La Chaux de Fonds, Switzerland. The IVS Archive (including the material from which *Volunteers for Peace* was compiled), is held at the County Record Office for Leicestershire: if it is moved, that office will be able to say where it has gone to.

INDEX